Marriage Conflicts

Marriage Conflicts

Resources
for Strategic Pastoral Counseling

Everett L. Worthington, Jr.
and Douglas McMurry

 Baker Books

A Division of Baker Book House Co
Grand Rapids, Michigan 49516

Published by Baker Books,
a division of Baker Book House Company
PO Box 6287, Grand Rapids, Michigan 49516-6287

Printed in the United States of America

Library of Congress Cataloging-in-Publication Data

Worthington, Everett L., 1946–
    Marriage conflicts: resources for strategic pastoral counseling/Everett L. Worthington, Jr. and Douglas McMurry.
    p. cm.
    Includes bibliographical references.
    ISBN 0-8010-9723-1
    1. Marriage counseling. 2. Pastoral counseling. 3. Marriage—Religious aspects—Christianity. I. McMurry, Douglas. II. Title.
BV4012.27.W669 1994
259'.1—dc20   93–39344

To Fred, Dale, Jim, and Don
Christian friends, ministers, and my counselors
—ELW

To Rev. Leonard Evans and Rev. Gary Smalley,
two pastors who showed me how to love my wife
in Jesus' name
—DM

Contents

Part 3 Application

An Introduction to Strategic Pastoral Counseling

David G. Benner

While the provision of spiritual counsel has been an integral part of Christian soul care since the earliest days of the church, the contemporary understanding and practice of pastoral counseling is largely a product of the twentieth century. Developing within the shadow of the modern psychotherapies, pastoral counseling has derived much of its style and approach from these clinical therapeutics. What this has meant is that pastoral counselors have often seen themselves more as counselors than as pastors and the counseling that they have provided has often been a rather awkward adaptation of clinical counseling models to a pastoral context. This, in turn, has often resulted in significant tension between the pastoral and psychological dimensions of the counseling provided by clergy and others in Christian ministry. It is also frequently reflected in pastoral counselors who are more interested in anything connected with the modern mystery cult of psychotherapy than with their own tradition of Christian soul care, and who, as a consequence, are often quite insecure in their pastoral role and identity.

9

While pastoral counseling owes much to the psychological culture that has gained ascendancy in the West during the past century, this influence has quite clearly been a mixed blessing. Contemporary pastoral counselors typically offer their help with much more psychological sophistication than was the case several decades ago, but all too often they do so without a clear sense of the uniqueness of counseling that is offered by a pastor. And not only are the distinctive spiritual resources of Christian ministry often deemphasized or ignored, but the tensions that are associated with attempts to directly translate clinical models of counseling into the pastoral context become a source of much frustration. This is in part why so many pastors report dissatisfaction with their counseling. While they indicate that this dissatisfaction is a result of insufficient training in and time for counseling, a bigger part of the problem may be that pastors have been offered approaches to counseling that are of questionable appropriateness for the pastoral context and that will inevitably leave them feeling frustrated and inadequate.

Strategic Pastoral Counseling is a model of counseling that has been specifically designed to fit the role, resources, and needs of the typical pastor who counsels. Information about this "typical" pastor was solicited by means of a survey of over 400 pastors (this research is described in the introductory volume of the series, *Strategic Pastoral Counseling: A Short-Term Structured Model* [Benner 1992]). The model appropriates the insights of contemporary counseling theory without sacrificing the resources of pastoral ministry. Furthermore, it takes its form and direction from the pastoral role and in so doing offers an approach to counseling that is not only congruent with the other aspects of pastoral ministry but that places pastoral counseling at the very heart of ministry.

The present volume represents an application of Strategic Pastoral Counseling to one commonly encountered problem situation. As such, it presupposes a familiarity with the basic model. Readers not familiar with *Strategic Pastoral Counseling: A Short-Term Structured Model* should consult this book for a detailed presentation of the model and its implementation. What follows is a brief review of this material which, while it does not adequately summarize all that is presented in that book, should serve as a reminder of the most important features of the Strategic Pastoral Counseling approach.

The Strategic Pastoral Counseling Model

Strategic Pastoral Counseling is short-term, bibliotherapeutic, wholistic, structured, spiritually focused, and explicitly Christian. Each of these characteristics will be briefly discussed in order.

Short-Term Counseling

Counseling can be brief (that is, conducted over a relatively few sessions), time-limited (that is, conducted within an initially fixed number of total sessions), or both. Strategic Pastoral Counseling is both brief and time-limited, working within a suggested maximum of five sessions. The decision to set this upper limit on the number of sessions was in response to the fact that the background research conducted in the design of the model indicated that 87 percent of the pastoral counseling conducted by pastors in general ministry involves five sessions or less. This short-term approach to counseling seems ideally suited to the time availability, training, and role demands of pastors.

Recent research in short-term counseling has made it clear that while such an approach requires that the counselor be diligent in maintaining the focus on the single agreed upon central problem, significant and enduring changes can occur through a very small number of counseling sessions. Strategic Pastoral Counseling differs, in this regard, from the more ongoing relationship of discipleship or spiritual guidance. In these, the goal is the development of spiritual maturity. Strategic Pastoral Counseling has a much more modest goal: examining a particular problem or experience in the light of God's will for and activity in the life of the individual seeking help and attempting to facilitate growth in and through that person's present life situation. While this is still an ambitious goal, its focused nature makes it quite attainable within a short period of time. It is this focus that makes the counseling strategic.

The five-session limit should be communicated by the pastor no later than the first session and preferably in the prior conversation when the time is set for this session. This ensures that the parishioner is aware of the time limit from the beginning and can share responsibility in keeping the counseling sessions focused. Some people will undoubtedly require more than five sessions in order to bring about a resolution of their problems. These people should be referred to someone who is appropriately qualified for such work; preparation for this referral will be one of the goals of the five sessions. However, the fact that such people may require more help than can be provided in five sessions of pastoral counseling does not mean that they cannot benefit from such focused short-term pastoral care; no individuals should be regarded as inappropriate candidates for Strategic Pastoral Counseling merely because they may require other help.

One final but important note about the suggested limit of five sessions is that this does not have to be tied to a corresponding period of five weeks. In fact, many pastors find weekly sessions to be less useful than sessions scheduled two or three weeks apart. This sort of spacing of the last couple of sessions is particularly helpful and should be considered even if the first several sessions are held weekly.

Bibliotherapeutic Counseling

Bibliotherapy refers to the therapeutic use of reading. Strategic Pastoral Counseling builds the use of written materials into the heart of its approach to pastoral caregiving. The Bible itself is, of course, a rich bibliotherapeutic resource and the encouragement of and direction in its reading is an important part of Strategic Pastoral Counseling. Its use must be disciplined and selective and particular care must be taken to ensure that it is never employed in a mechanical or impersonal manner. However, when used appropriately it can unquestionably be one of the most dynamic and powerful resources available to the pastor who counsels.

While the Bible is a unique bibliotherapeutic resource, it is not the only such resource. Strategic Pastoral Counseling comes with a built-in set of specifically designed resources. Each of the 10 volumes in this series has an accompanying book written for the parishioner who is being seen in counseling. These resource books are written by the same authors as the volumes for pastors and are designed for easy integration into counseling sessions.

The use of reading materials that are consistent with the counseling being provided can serve as a most significant support and extension of the counseling offered by a pastor. The parishioner now has a helping resource that is not limited by the pastor's time and availability. Furthermore, the pastor can now allow the written materials to do part of the work of counseling, using the sessions to deal with those matters that are not as well addressed through the written page.

Wholistic Counseling

It might seem surprising to suggest that a short-term counseling approach should also be wholistic. But this is both possible and highly desirable. Wholistic counseling is counseling that is responsive to the totality of the complex psycho-spiritual dynamics that make up the life of human persons. Biblical psychology is clearly a wholistic psychology. The various "parts" of persons (i.e., body, soul, spirit, heart, flesh, etc.) are never presented as separate faculties or independent components of persons but always as different ways of seeing the whole person. Biblical discussions of persons emphasize first and foremost their essential unity of being. Humans are ultimately understandable only in the light of this primary and irreducible wholeness and helping efforts that are truly Christian must resist the temptation to see persons only through their thoughts, feelings, behaviors, or any other single manifestation of being.

The alternative to wholism in counseling is to focus on only one of these modalities of functioning and this is, indeed, what many approaches to counseling do. In contrast, Strategic Pastoral Counseling asserts that pastoral counseling must be responsive to the behavioral (action), cognitive (thought), and affective (feeling) elements of personal functioning. Each examined separately can obscure that which is really going on with a person. But taken together they form the basis for a comprehensive assessment and effective intervention. Strategic Pastoral Counseling provides a framework for ensuring that each of these spheres of functioning is addressed and this, in fact, provides much of the structure for the counseling.

Structured Counseling

The structured nature of Strategic Pastoral Counseling is that which enables its brevity, ensuring that each of the sessions has a clear focus and that each builds upon the previous ones in contributing toward the accomplishment of the overall goals. The framework that structures Strategic Pastoral Counseling is sufficiently tight as to enable the pastor to provide a wholistic assessment and counseling intervention within a maximum of five sessions and yet it is also sufficiently flexible to allow for differences in individual styles of different counselors. This is very important because Strategic Pastoral Counseling is not primarily a set of techniques but an intimate encounter of and dialogue between people.

The structure of Strategic Pastoral Counseling grows out of the goal of addressing the feelings, thoughts, and behaviors that are part of the troubling experiences of the person seeking help. It is also a structure that is responsive to the several tasks that face the pastoral counselor, tasks such as conducting an initial assessment, developing a general understanding of the problem and of the person's major needs, and selecting and delivering interventions and resources that will bring help. This structure is described in more detail later.

Spiritually Focused Counseling

The fourth distinctive of Strategic Pastoral Counseling is that it is spiritually focused. This does not mean that only religious matters are discussed. Our spirituality is our essential heart commitments, our basic life direction, and our fundamental allegiances. These spiritual aspects of our being are, of course, reflected in our attitudes toward God and are expressed in our explicitly religious values and behaviors. However, they are also reflected in matters that may seem on the surface to be much less religious. Strategic

Pastoral Counselors place a primacy on listening to this underlying spiritual story. They listen for what we might call the story behind the story.

But listening to the story behind the story requires that one first listen to and take seriously the presenting story. To disregard the presenting situation is spiritualization of a problem. It fails to take the problem seriously and makes a mockery of counseling as genuine dialogue. The Strategic Pastoral Counselor thus listens to and enters into the experience of parishioners as they relate their struggles and life's experiences. But while this is a real part of the story, it is not the whole story that must be heard and understood. For in the midst of this story emerges another: the story of their spiritual response to these experiences. This response may be one of unwavering trust in God but a failure to expect much of him. Or it may be one of doubt, anger, confusion, or despair. Each of these is a spiritual response to present struggles and in one form or another, the spiritual aspect of the person's experience will always be discernible to the pastor who watches for it. Strategic Pastoral Counseling makes this underlying spiritual story the primary focus.

Explicitly Christian Counseling

While it is important to not confuse spirituality with religiosity, it is equally important to not confuse Christian spirituality with any of its imitations. In this regard, it is crucial that Strategic Pastoral Counseling be distinctively and explicitly Christian. And while Strategic Pastoral Counseling begins with a focus on spiritual matters understood broadly, its master goal is to facilitate the other person's awareness of and response to the call of God to surrender and service. This is the essential and most important distinctive of Strategic Pastoral Counseling.

One of the ways in which Strategic Pastoral Counseling is made explicitly Christian is through its utilization of Christian theological language, images, and concepts and the religious resources of prayer, Scripture, and the sacraments. These resources must never be used in a mechanical, legalistic, or magical fashion. But used sensitively and wisely, they can be the conduit for a dynamic contact between God and the person seeking pastoral help. And this is the goal of their utilization, not some superficial baptizing of the counseling in order to make it Christian but rather a way of bringing the one seeking help more closely in touch with the God who is the source of all life, growth, and healing.

Another important resource that is appropriated by the Strategic Pastoral Counselor is that of the church as a community. Too often pastoral counseling is conducted in a way that is not appreciably different from that which might be offered by a Christian counselor in private practice. This most unfortunate practice ignores the rich resources that are potentially available in any Christian congregation. One of the most important ways in which Strategic Pastoral Counseling is able to maintain its short-term nature is by the pastor connecting the person seeking help with others in the church who can provide portions of that help. The congregation can, of course, also be involved in less individualistic ways. Support and ministry groups of various sorts are becoming a part of many congregations that seek to provide a dynamic ministry to their community and are potentially important resources for the Strategic Pastoral Counselor.

A final and even more fundamental way in which Strategic Pastoral Counseling is Christian is in the reliance that it encourages on the Holy Spirit. The Spirit is the indispensable source of all wisdom that is necessary for the practice of pastoral counseling. Recognizing that all healing and growth are ultimately of God, the Strategic Pastoral Counselor can thus take comfort in this reliance on the Spirit of God and on the fact that ultimate responsibility for people and their well-being lies with God.

Stages and Tasks of Strategic Pastoral Counseling

The three overall stages that organize Strategic Pastoral Counseling can be described as *encounter, engagement,* and *disengagement.* The first stage of Strategic Pastoral Counseling, encounter, corresponds to the initial session in which the goal is to establish personal contact with the person seeking help, set the boundaries for the counseling relationship, become acquainted with that person and the central concerns, conduct a pastoral diagnosis, and develop a mutually acceptable focus for the subsequent sessions. The second stage, engagement, involves the pastor moving beyond the first contact and establishing a deeper working alliance with the person seeking help. This normally occupies the next one to three sessions and entails the exploration of the person's feelings, thoughts, and behavioral patterns associated with this problem area and the development of new perspectives and strategies for coping or change. The third and final stage, disengagement, describes the focus of the last one or possibly two sessions, and involves an evaluation of progress and an assessment of remaining concerns, the making of a referral for further help if this is needed, and the ending of the counseling relationship. These stages and tasks are summarized in the table below.

Stages and Tasks of Strategic Pastoral Counseling

Stage 1: Encounter (Session 1)
  * Joining and boundary-setting
  * Exploring the central concerns and relevant history
  * Conducting a pastoral diagnosis
  * Achieving a mutually agreeable focus for counseling

Stage 2: Engagement (Sessions 2, 3, 4)
  * Exploration of cognitive, affective, and behavioral aspects of the problem and the identification of resources for coping or change

Stage 3: Disengagement (Sessions 4, 5)
  * Evaluation of progress and assessment of remaining concerns
  * Referral (if needed)
  * Termination of counseling

The Encounter Stage

The first task in this initial stage of Strategic Pastoral Counseling is joining and boundary-setting. Joining involves putting the parishioner at ease by means of a few moments of casual conversation that is designed to ease pastor and parishioner into contact. Such preliminary conversation should never take more than five minutes and should usually be kept to two or three. It will not always be necessary, because some people are immediately ready to tell their story. Boundary-setting involves the communication of the purpose of this session and the time frame for the session and your work together. This should not normally require more than a sentence or two.

The exploration of central concerns and relevant history usually begins with an invitation for parishioners to describe what led them to seek help at the present time. After hearing an expression of these immediate concerns, it is usually helpful to get a brief historical perspective on these concerns and the person. Ten to 15 minutes of exploration of the course of development of the presenting problems and their efforts to cope or get help with them is the foundation of this part of the session. It is also important at this point to get some idea of the parishioner's present living and family arrangements as well as work and/or educational situation. The organizing thread for this section of the first interview should be the presenting problem. These matters will not be the only ones discussed but this focus serves to give the session the necessary direction.

Stripped of its distracting medical connotations, diagnosis is problem definition and this is a fundamental part of any approach to counseling. Diagnoses involve judgments about the nature of the problem and, either implicitly or explicitly, pastoral counselors make such judgments every time they commence a counseling relationship. But in order for diagnoses to be relevant they must guide the counseling that will follow. This means that the categories of pastoral assessment must be primarily related to the spiritual focus, which is foundational to any counseling that is appropriately called pastoral. Thus, the diagnosis called for in the first stage of Strategic Pastoral Counseling involves an assessment of the person's spiritual well-being.

The framework for pastoral diagnosis adopted by Strategic Pastoral Counseling is that suggested by Malony (1988) and used as the basis of his Religious Status Interview. Malony proposed that the diagnosis of Christian religious well-being should involve the assessment of the person's awareness of God, acceptance of God's grace, repentance and responsibility, response to God's leadership and direction, involvement in the church, experience of fellowship, ethics, and openness in the faith. While this approach to pastoral diagnosis has been found to be helpful by many, the Strategic Pastoral Counselor need not feel confined by it. It is offered as a suggested framework for conducting a pastoral assessment and each individual pastoral counselor needs to approach this task in ways that fit his or her own theological convictions and personal style. Further details on conducting a pastoral assessment can be found in *Strategic Pastoral Counseling: A Short-Term Structured Model*.

The final task of the encounter stage of Strategic Pastoral Counseling is achieving a mutually agreeable focus for counseling. Often this is self-evident, made immediately clear by the first expression of the parishioner. At other times parishioners will report a wide range of concerns in the first session and will have to be asked what should constitute the primary problem focus. The identification of the primary problem focus leads naturally to a formulation of goals for the counseling. These goals will sometimes be quite specific (i.e., to be able to make an informed decision about a potential job change) but will also at times be rather broad (i.e., to be able to express feelings related to an illness). As is illustrated in these examples, some goals will describe an end-point while others will describe more of a process. Maintaining this flexibility in how goals are understood is crucial if Strategic Pastoral Counseling is to be a helpful counseling approach for the broad range of situations faced by the pastoral counselor.

The Engagement Stage

The second stage of Strategic Pastoral Counseling involves the further engagement of the pastor and the one seeking help around the problems and concerns that brought them together. This is the heart of the counseling process. The major tasks of this stage are the exploration of the person's feelings, thoughts, and behavioral patterns associated with the central concerns and the development of new perspectives and strategies for coping or change.

It is important to note that the work of this stage may well begin in the first session. The model should not be interpreted in a rigid or mechanical manner. If the goals of the first stage are completed with time remaining in the first session, one can very appropriately begin to move into the tasks of this next stage. However, once the tasks of Stage 1 are completed, those associated with this second stage become the central focus. If the full five sessions of Strategic Pastoral Counseling are employed, this second stage normally provides the structure for sessions 2, 3, and 4.

The central foci for the three sessions normally associated with this stage are the feelings, thoughts, and behaviors associated with the problem presented by the person seeking help. Although these are usually intertwined, a selective focus on each, one at a time, ensures that each is adequately addressed and that all the crucial dynamics of the person's psychospiritual functioning are considered.

The reason for beginning with feelings is that this is where most people themselves begin when they come to a counselor. But this does not mean that most people know their feelings. The exploration of feelings involves encouraging people to face and express whatever it is that they are feeling, to the end that these feelings can be known and then dealt with appropriately. The goal at this point is to listen and respond empathically to the feelings of those seeking help, not to try to change them.

After an exploration of the major feelings being experienced by the person seeking help, the next task is an exploration of the thoughts associated with these feelings and the development of alternative ways of understanding present experiences. It is in this phase of Strategic Pastoral Counseling that the explicit use of Scripture is usually most appropriate. Bearing in mind the potential misuses and problems that can be associated with such use of religious resources, the pastoral counselor should be, nonetheless, open to a direct presentation of scriptural truths when they offer the possibility of a new and helpful perspective on one's situation.

The final task of the engagement stage of Strategic Pastoral Counseling grows directly out of this work on understanding and involves the exploration of the behavioral components of the person's functioning. Here the pastor explores what concrete things the person is doing in the face of the problems or distressing situations being encountered and together with the parishioner begins to identify changes in behavior that may be desirable. The goal of this stage is to identify changes that both pastor and parishioner agree are important and to begin to establish concrete strategies for making these changes.

The Disengagement Stage

The last session or two involves preparation for the termination of counseling and includes two specific tasks: the evaluation of progress and assessment of remaining concerns, and making arrangements regarding a referral if this is needed.

The evaluation of progress is usually a process that both pastor and parishioner will find rewarding. Some of this may be done during previous sessions. Even when this is the case, it is a good idea to use the last session to undertake a brief review of what has been learned from the counseling. Closely associated with this, of course, is an identification of remaining concerns. Seldom is everything resolved after five sessions. This means that the parishioner is preparing to leave counseling with some work yet to be done. But he or she does so with plans for the future and the development of these is an important task of the disengagement stage of Strategic Pastoral Counseling.

If significant problems remain at this point, the last couple of sessions should also be used to make referral arrangements. Ideally these should be discussed in the second or third session and they should by now be all arranged. It might even be ideal if by this point the parishioner could have had a first session with the new counselor, thus allowing a processing of this first experience as part of the final pastoral counseling session.

Recognition of one's own limitations of time, experience, training, and ability is an indispensable component of the practice of all professionals. Pastors are no exception. Pastors offering Strategic Pastoral Counseling need, therefore, to be aware of the resources within their community and be prepared to refer parishioners for help that they can better receive elsewhere.

In the vast majority of cases, the actual termination of a Strategic Pastoral Counseling relationship goes very smoothly. Most often both pastor and parishioner agree that there is no further need to meet and they find easy agreement with, even if some sadness around, the decision to discontinue the counseling sessions. However, there may be times when this process is somewhat difficult. This will sometimes be due to the parishioner's desire to continue to meet. At other times the difficulty in terminating will reside within the pastor. Regardless, the best course of action is usually to follow through on the initial limits agreed upon by both parties.

The exception to this rule is a situation where the parishioner is facing some significant stress or crisis at the end of the five sessions and where there are no other available resources to provide the support needed. If this is the situation, an extension of a few sessions may be appropriate. However, this should again be time-limited and should take the form of crisis management. It should not involve more sessions than is absolutely necessary to restore some degree of stability or to introduce the parishioner to other people who can be of assistance.

Conclusion

Strategic Pastoral Counseling provides a framework for pastors who seek to counsel in a way that is congruent with the rest of their pastoral responsibilities, psychologically informed and responsible. While skill in implementing the model comes only over time, because the approach is focused and time-limited it is quite possible for most pastors to acquire these skills. However, counseling skills cannot be adequately learned simply by reading books. As with all interpersonal skills, they must be learned through practice, and ideally, this practice is best acquired in a context of supervisory feedback from a more experienced pastoral counselor.

The pastor who has mastered the skills of Strategic Pastoral Counseling is in a position to proclaim the Word of God in a highly personalized and relevant manner to people who are often desperate for help. This is a unique and richly rewarding opportunity. Rather than scattering seed in a broadcast manner across ground that is often stony and hard even if at places it is also fertile and receptive to growth, the pastoral counselor has the opportunity to carefully plant one seed at a time. Knowing the soil conditions, he or she is also able to plant it in a highly individualized manner, taking pains to ensure that it will not be quickly blown away, and then gently watering and nourishing its growth. This is the unique opportunity for the ministry of Strategic Pastoral Counseling. It is my prayer that pastors will see the centrality of counseling to their call to ministry, feel encouraged by the presence of an approach to pastoral counseling that lies within their skills and time availability, and will take up these responsibilities with renewed vigor and clarity of direction.

Preface

This book is aimed at helping pastors counsel effectively.

Despite its clear focus on marital counseling, it may benefit others. The counselor within a pastoral counseling agency might share a similar perspective, though more time might be available for counseling than is available for the typical congregational pastor. The lay Christian counselor might also benefit from this book. Generally, lay counselors, like pastors, face time constraints and may wish to counsel within an explicitly Christian framework without employing a professional model of counseling. Finally, Christian professionals may want to shape their marital counseling around more explicitly Christian principles than their graduate training afforded them. We hope this book will aid the integration of Christianity into their practice. Like water running downhill, psychological and emotional problems usually follow a predictable course. When people have a problem, they try to use their personal resources to solve it. Most of the time, they are eventually successful.

When they are unable to solve the problem, they usually seek help from a family member or close friend. Usually, the family member or friend will listen to the problem, give some good advice, and support attempts to employ the advice. Most of the time, the problem is solved; sometimes it isn't.

In that event, distressed people may seek help from someone else, usually an effective lay helper. If that person can't help, individuals—especially if they are Christians—may then seek help from a pastor. Sometimes the pastor can't help either. People may then seek help from a mental health professional.

The counseling employed by the trained mental health professional is different from nonprofessional counseling. It generally employs a systematic assault on a person's problem using recognized counseling theories and techniques, repetition, weekly meetings over a number of months, clearly bounded counseling hours (each session usually lasts 50 minutes), and direct fees for counseling services (which might be completely or partially paid for by insurance companies). Unlike most other forms of helping, psychotherapy or professional counseling doesn't offer advice. Frankly, by the time most clients reach the professional's office, they have usually heard or thought of any advice that the professional might give. Like other forms of helping, professional counseling is effective for most people (Strupp, Hadley, and Gomez-Schwartz 1977). About 5 percent of people in professional counseling may get worse, and some people may not change as a result of professional counseling. Most, however, get better faster and improve more than people who do not have professional counseling.

Most pastors who counsel have looked to professional counseling for their models of how to counsel. In the 1950s and 1960s Carl Rogers (1951, 1957), with his emphasis on unconditional acceptance of the client, was the hero of many pastoral counselors. They based their methods and goals on Rogers' professional model. During the 1970s and 1980s pastors drew from other professional models for their counseling. Among them were Transactional Analysis, Jungian therapy, and cognitive therapy, which has proved to be especially attractive to evangelical Christians because the rationality of cognitive therapy is compatible with a rational, biblically based approach to Christianity.

Adapting the professional model for pastoral counseling has been made easier within the past two decades because of the rise of Christian professional counselors, who have adapted various forms of professional psychotherapy and counseling to fit a religiously compatible framework. Nonetheless, there are fundamental problems with most Christianized counseling theories. Such models—and Worthington's (1989) model of marriage counseling is one—rely on a professional source of authority and were designated for use over a longer time frame than is available to most pastors.

Pastors have a unique authority. Scripture shows us that the mature Christian is called to counsel the distressed. Scriptural authority undergirds counseling by pastors.

Pastors are generally called into ministry; they are then expected to mature quickly so that they can counsel wisely. Through time and experience, pastors learn to live by faith working through love. Then, through their hard-won maturity in living out their faith, pastors are equipped to teach their parishioners how to live out their faith.

This book presents a model of counseling that is aimed directly at the pastor. It provides a three-step strategy for dealing with marriage difficulties, which is expanded to a five-session model. (The pastor may, of course, lengthen or shorten the model to fit his or her own constraints and those of his or her parishioner.[1]) Counseling techniques are discussed but are not emphasized. We believe that the typical pastor has a wealth of practical counseling experience, and thus counseling techniques, on which to draw. With a viable strategy, such as we outline in this book, the pastor can use the techniques with which he or she is already comfortable (or consult other books on professional and pastoral marriage counseling) to help his or her parishioners grow in their faith while they deal with their marital difficulties.

---

1. Throughout this book we use "he or she" and "his or her" to refer to individual pastors. This reflects the reality that both men and women serve as pastors. It is not a theological position on whether both men and women *should* be pastors.

Part 1

Overview of Strategic Pastoral Counseling for Marriage Conflicts

1

The Need for Strategic Pastoral Marital Counseling

Marla cowered in her chair, like a dog that has been abused so often that it whines at the sight of a human. Les, meanwhile, sat rigidly—an ice sculpture, seemingly sturdy but inherently fragile. Their pastor, Dennis, listened to Marla's story, cringing at the knowledge that he would soon have to do something besides make comforting sounds.

I could tell them that things will get better, Dennis thought, *but I'm not sure they will. I could tell them to let go and trust God, but would they? Could they? For 10 years, I've pastored this church. I've seen Marla and Les destroy each other. I've preached sermons at them, talked to them, counseled them, wept over them, and enjoyed the occasional good times with them. Despite my efforts, here they sit with ravaged self-esteem, blasted by thousands of explosions through the years. They have battled and I've stood beside them on the battle lines. Now they are war weary. They want a divorce.*

Dennis felt despair wash over him. *I need to give them hope, but I don't know what to do. I was trained to be a preacher and a good listener, not a marriage therapist. The Lord can't expect me to handle this.*

The final straw for both Marla and Les had been Les's latest drinking binge. On Friday, he had stopped at the local bar for a drink, even though he had promised Marla that he wouldn't drink again. One drink had led to another, and Les hadn't come home Friday—or Saturday—night. Sunday afternoon, he had finally dragged in. That night, Marla had found another woman's underwear in the car. When she had confronted Les, he couldn't even remember the weekend.

Now, it was Monday, and though it was supposed to be Pastor Dennis's day off, Marla and Les needed help. *What can I say? What can I do?* In times like these Pastor Dennis doubted his call to the ministry.

Many People Seek Marital Counseling from Pastors

Pastor Dennis's plight is common. Surveys have found that over 60 percent of Americans prefer to see clergy about personal problems (Gurin, Veroff, and Feld 1960; Veroff, Kulka, and Douvan 1981). The most common problem presented to pastors (Arnold and Schick 1979; Worthington 1986) and Christian mental health professionals (Worthington, et al. 1988) is marital trouble, followed closely by family difficulties, which may include marital tensions.

The demand for individual and marital counseling from pastors is likely to increase. One reason for the likely increase is economic. Insurance companies almost never reimburse psychotherapists for marital counseling because marital distress is not considered a health problem. The cost of therapy from professionals can range from $60 to $125 per hour. For most people, that is prohibitively high. Most pastors don't charge for counseling.

Another reason for a likely increase in demand for pastoral counseling is a growing sense of spirituality in modern Western culture. People increasingly sense their need for "something more," and vainly try to fill the need with groups such as women's and men's support groups or twelve-step programs. Many people return to the church for "something more," further increasing the typical pastor's counseling load.

A third reason for the likely increase in pastoral counseling is a continually rising divorce rate. Despite several short periods of flat rate of divorce, such as the one we are currently in (Lasswell and Lasswell 1991; U.S. Bureau of the Census 1984), the divorce rate has risen exponentially since 1870 (Cherlin 1981). Of course, it cannot increase indefinitely, but it may not have peaked yet. Marriages continue to feel the strain, and many couples who desperately try to stave off divorce seek counseling.

There are many reasons for the increase in the divorce rate. First, modern culture has become increasingly individualistic, which has eroded the foundation of mutual self-sacrifice needed for long-term marriage. Furthermore, happiness has become the primary value of modern society. When marital tensions rise, people, pursuing happiness, often run from their pain.

Second, medical breakthroughs have led to longer life expectancies. As people live longer, they spend proportionately more of their lives with a mate and less rearing children, which provides additional opportunities for weak marriages to become destructive divorces.

Third, the world has become increasingly fast-paced and stressful. Stress turns people's attention inward and undermines a concern for others.

Fourth, marital norms have changed. Remarriage has multiplied in response to the increasing divorce rate (Walsh 1991). Remarriage has a substantially higher rate of divorce than does first marriage (Cherlin 1981), increasing the overall instability of marriage. Nonmarital cohabitation has also increased, spurred by a high divorce rate and social trends toward individualism (Bumpass, Sweet, and Cherlin 1991; DeMaris and Rao 1992; Schoen 1992; Thompson and Colella 1992). The rate of divorce for couples who have cohabited has consistently been found to be greater than the rate of divorce for couples who have not cohabited.

In summary, the demand for marriage counseling in general and marriage counseling from pastors in particular is likely to increase in the future.

The Supply of Pastors Available to Counsel Is Dwindling

Organized religion, especially within mainline Protestant churches, is declining (Marsden 1990; Wuthnow 1988). The number of clergy available per congregant is decreasing even more rapidly than is the number of people who attend religious services (Wuthnow 1988). This will have at least two effects on pastors who counsel.

First, with the rising demand for counseling and a dwindling supply of pastors who counsel, the counseling caseload of pastors is rising. Second, pastors must perform duties besides pastoral counseling—pastoral care, teaching, preaching, and administration. Thus, the time available for counseling is shrinking.

Pastors' Training in Marital Counseling Is Inadequate

Most pastors receive little seminary training in counseling (Worthington 1986). They generally are trained in listening skills, which helps little in dealing with specialized situations. During training, actual counseling is often limited to Clinical Pastoral Education (CPE), which involves writing transcripts of hospital visits and discussing the personal and spiritual growth of the pastor. Most CPE programs have little relevance to marital counseling.

Marriage counseling is a specialized situation—especially when both spouses are present. Listening skills alone fail the marital counselor. The aggressiveness with which most troubled couples converse or argue often intimidates even the experienced individual counselor. When one spouse stops talking, the other spouse begins. The pastor who waits for both spouses to finish talking or simply reflects what each says will spend his or her time merely listening to the couple fight and feeling inadequate as a helper.

Marriage counseling requires the pastor to maintain the trust of two people who often have lost trust in each other and have lost hope in solving their problems. These troubled spouses may have emotional disturbances, problems in childrearing, and other conflicts. War is likely to break out over the slightest provocation and retaliation is often immediate and damaging.

Self-Training Is Often Necessary

There is little postseminary training available for the typical pastor to build skills in marital counseling. An occasional workshop at a conference might be the only training in marriage counseling he or she receives. The pastor is left with the task of educating himself or herself through reading books about counseling.

These books often are deficient for effective self-training for several reasons. First, the books may be excellent professional treatises, but they may not share the value system of the committed Christian. They may advocate techniques that are not acceptable to Christians or may be based on presuppositions antagonistic to Christianity. Second, the books may be excellent Christian books about marriage or divorce but do not deal with how to counsel distressed couples. Finally, a few Christian professional counselors have articulated versions of marital therapy that are generally consistent with Christian principles. Nonetheless, many attempts to integrate psychology and Christianity are not as useful as they could be to the practicing pastor because they assume a professional model of counseling—one that the typical pastor does not have the training, mentality, time, or desire to employ. The pastor must work diligently to adapt the professional model to his or her everyday use.

Pressures from the Legal Front

Because they have received little training in marriage counseling, pastors are often intimidated by the litigious tenor of the times. Even pastors giving counsel to parishioners are not immune from lawsuits, as the recent case at Rev. John MacArthur's Word of Grace Church showed. Even though the counselor was not found to be financially responsible for damages in that case, the case increased the possibility of litigation in pastoral counseling because of the attention to it. Fear of litigation could dissuade many pastors from offering marital counsel, especially those pastors who feel ill-prepared to counsel competently.

Needed: Strategic Pastoral Marital Counseling

These converging trends argue for an effective, practical method of conducting marital counseling within a Christian framework, an approach that is tailored specifically to pastors who counsel.

In the following chapters, we define a strategy for helping people improve their marriages. The strategy is carried out within three stages of pastoral counseling: encounter, engagement, and disengagement. We recommend five sessions for carrying out the strategy, but we encourage pastors to adapt the three-stage strategy to fit their counselee(s) and time constraints. We suggest guidelines about how to carry out the three stages within a five-session format and describe plans for each session. Finally, we report case studies to show how the method might be applied.

2

The Strategy
and the Model

A strategy is an overall battle plan. A model is an understanding about the method by which the strategy will be employed within different stages of the battle.

The Strategy

God has a decisive pattern for living and solving problems: *faith working through love* (Gal. 5:6).

Faith working through love is the New Testament nutshell description of the Christian life. A mature Christian is one who is learning to live out this pattern in every area of life. The purpose of this book is to help pastors equip their people to live out this pattern in their marriages. Marriage is the acid test of discipleship. We can fudge our Christianity everywhere but at home. At home, we are forced to deal with basic, ingrained patterns of self-centeredness—patterns that have not yet come under the lordship of Jesus Christ.

Jesus Christ sometimes uses marital problems to expose sin that he wishes to root out of us. Marital problems can force us to look more deeply into our personal discipleship. In short, marital problems are discipleship challenges.

We define pastoral counseling in terms of disciple-making. For too long, pastors have modeled their ministry after secular helping professions, which are often guided by concepts and morals that do not come from the Bible. But pastoral counseling that pursues faith working through love fits with the Great Commission to the church, putting pastoral counseling in its proper place in Christian ministry. In this understanding of marital counseling, preaching, counseling, and small-group disciple-making fit together and support each other. All aspects of Christian ministry are aimed at a common goal: making mature disciples who exemplify faith working through love. Jesus helps us when we want what he wants. We bring in God's kingdom when we counsel in harmony with God's will in the power of the Holy Spirit.

Pastors can offer the hope of marital discipleship to their people. It is a pastor's job, privilege, and holy calling to invite his or her people to believe in the Christian pattern and to practice it in the intimacy of marriage. This is the true calling of the church, of every pastor, and of the marriage counselor who operates within the church.

The pastor employs this principle—faith working through love—to help the couple or individual with marital problems solve the problems. The pastor helps distressed people understand and apply to their marriage the principle of faith working through love. He or she does this by direct teaching, training the couple in righteousness, stimulating practice at forgiving their spouse for perceived wrongs, helping spouses forgive parents and others in their past for contributing to the roots of relationship problems, and modeling faith working through love in the entire pastoral ministry.

Definitions

Faith is "being sure of what we hope for and certain of what we do not see" (Heb. 11:1). Jesus can heal troubled marriages. This is often not seen by troubled couples, who see only pain and anger.

Building the conviction that Jesus can and wants to heal their marriage can build their faith. The pastor promotes faith by bringing faith and hope into a situation that marriage partners see as hopeless. By maintaining an attitude of faith and by working with the couple through love, the pastor can help make the couple "certain of what [they] do not see."

Love is exercising the will to value and to avoid devaluing people. The pastor wants to promote self-sacrificial *agapē* love. Jesus loved us. As he told in the parable of the hidden treasure (Matt. 13:44), we were a treasure buried in a field. Jesus found that treasure and sold everything he had on earth (his life) to buy the treasure. He *agapē* loved us, so we can *agapē* love others (1 John 3:16; 4:10).

The basic task in a marriage, then, is for spouses to consistently love (will to value and not devalue) each other, which will build trust and security and will provide a basis for solving practical problems.

That task is evident in all aspects of marriage. In establishing a balance of intimacy and privacy, both partners seek to value each other. In communicating important aspects of their worlds, both partners seek to value each other. In resolving differences over money, in-laws, sex, chores, childrearing practices, and the like, both partners seek to value each other. In confessing their failings and forgiving the partner's transgressions or in forging a mutual understanding of the marriage, both partners seek to value each other. In adhering to a lifelong commitment to marriage and to working to make the marriage better, both partners seek to value each other. Love is the primary task of marriage.

How the Pastor Helps

To help partners love each other more, the pastor must help the couple explore the problem—both the root in the past and the fruit in the present.

The *past root* usually involves relationships with the parents, especially things learned before the child was old enough to reason clearly about marital relationships. Other roots of devaluing or of failing to value the partner can occur in previous male-female relationships during dating or a previous marriage. From past relationships, each spouse develops ways of not consistently valuing or only intermittently valuing the spouse.

The *present fruit* includes ways that partners currently treat each other. They may fail to value or actively devalue each other. In either case, there is a failure to love the partner with the *agapē* love born of God, and thus the marriage will suffer.

One goal of pastoral counseling, then, is to help spouses love and depend on God rather than act on what others—whether parents or previous romantic partners—have taught them to do.

The Cause of Marital Problems

Problems in marriage arise when partners do not value each other or actively devalue each other.

In marriage, people commit to value each other. In fact, the commitment is a particularly important type of commitment, a covenant lasting until death. The lifelong challenge in the marriage covenant is continually to find ways to value each other. Issues about which spouses differ (finances, in-law relations, child discipline) are not important in themselves. These are merely occasions of challenge in which love can grow, but in which love can be bruised if partners fail to value each other.

When people do not feel valued, they may feel sad, angry, jealous, depressed, resentful, or bitter. They may deal with the emotions in the flesh or in faith. When people deal with the emotions in the flesh, the emotions often grow and transmute into even uglier emotions. When people deal with the emotions in faith, they work through love to heal the bruised emotions and promote an increased sense of value in the partner.

When people do not feel valued, they also act—either in the flesh or in faith. In the flesh, they may desperately seek assurance of valuing, working hard and sacrificing their own dignity at times to get evidence of their value from the spouse. Or, they may seek revenge, become self-preoccupied, or withdraw from the marriage psychologically or physically. They may attack, devaluing the spouse to elevate their own value. It is nearly impossible to wrest a sense of valuing from an unwilling partner. It is impossible to bludgeon—either psychologically or physically—a sense of valuing from a defensive, hurt partner. Only through faith can a sense of value be won. God can give the grace for one spouse to value the partner even if the partner is hurting or devaluing the spouse. Then, as one partner begins to value the other, love can grow in the other. God can soften both spouses' hearts to make them receptive to mutual valuing.

When people do not feel valued, they blame the spouse, God, and sometimes themselves. They focus on their own pain and become self-centered, evaluating almost everything in terms of the impact it will have on them. As they think negatively, they will respond either in the flesh or in faith. In the flesh, thoughts feed on themselves, attracting other negative thoughts like a shark feeding frenzy. In faith, God helps the person "take captive every thought to make it obedient to Christ" (2 Cor. 10:5b).

The Solution to Marital Problems

If the root of marital problems is insufficient valuing or too much devaluing in one or both partners, the solution to them, then, is to help the partners attribute and show more value to each other and thus feel more valued.

The pastor is in a good position to promote this. The pastor may shore up the value of people by: (1) referring to Jesus and Scripture as the basis for correcting wrong concepts about God; (2) placing people within the context of a valuing Christian community (which usually means involving them with small groups of people within the congregation); (3) behaving lovingly toward people; (4) being a good example; and (5) dealing with the past roots and present fruits of their problems intentionally and systematically.

People can choose to love through faith, even if they feel at the time that their partner is unlovable. Loving feelings follow acts of faith. Acts of faith usually follow a belief that faith-full acts are desirable, and honor God, our spouse, and ourselves.

When people are distressed because they don't feel sufficiently valued by their partner, they can attempt to bring about change in two ways: by manipulation or by faith working through love. The pastor must model faith working through love and help the partners want to give up manipulation.

Faith working through love is, thus, active. To receive valuing from the partner, the person must act in faith, based on value already received from Jesus. Faith-initiated and faith-sustained behaviors can then convey that one values the partner. The person does not wait passively to receive a gift of valuing from the partner. This is a paradox of Christianity. People receive God's gift of love, then give love away, receiving even more love back from others "pressed down, shaken together and running over" (Luke 6:38).

The general counseling strategy is to help each person, by faith, value the partner more than previously. The pastor accomplishes this strategy through modeling, teaching, training, and discipling people to apply the faith-acting-through-love principle to the marriage.

The Model

Strategic Pastoral Counseling occurs in three stages: encounter, engagement, and disengagement.

The band begins to play a lilting waltz. The young man spies an attractive woman across the room. He ambles over, chats with her, extends his hand, and asks her to dance. This is the encounter stage.

They walk onto the dance floor, fall into each other's arms, and waltz around the floor, weaving among couples, turning, swaying, avoiding collisions. This is the engagement stage.

The music ends, the partners applaud the band and each other, and casually chat as the man escorts the woman back to her seat. Yet both are changed by their encounter. They thank each other and part, thinking of their exhilarating movement together and trying not to recall that he stepped on her foot. They feel enriched despite that bittersweet moment. This is the disengagement stage.

Counseling is like a dance. The pastor leads the dance steps, but smooth progress depends on the pastor and counselee establishing a mutual rhythm that allows them to negotiate the dance floor. As with dancing, there are patterned moves. The pastor knows effective counseling techniques, which he or she may use. Yet obstacles may rise up—like a logjam of other couples at one place on the dance floor—to prevent the completion of the dance. The counselee may have well-established ways of reacting in marriage, but the pastor must still lead new dance steps.

The Stages in Brief

In pastoral counseling, the *encounter* stage involves two major tasks: (1) establishing and maintaining a working relationship in which counseling is initiated and structured and the pastor joins the partner or couple to attempt to solve the marriage problem; and (2) assessing the appropriate targets for change. In each task, the pastor shows that he or she values the partner or couple and attempts to promote more valuing love between partners.

Engagement involves exploring feelings, thoughts, and behaviors in past relationships and in the present relationship. It involves a healing of both memories and current relationships. It also involves building new patterns of acting, thinking, and feeling both toward the partner and toward God. Engagement focuses the partner's or couple's efforts on changing their Christian values or beliefs, closeness, communication, conflict resolution strategies, cognition about the marriage (i.e., their tendency to blame each other and God), confession and forgiveness, or commitment. In each area of their marriage, they strive to devalue the partner less and value the partner more.

Disengagement involves consolidating changes within the marriage as well as helping partners remain involved in the Christian community so they will continue to feel valued. Unlike the professional counselor, who sees the client only during the 50-minute counseling hour, the pastor interacts with most partners in a variety of ways, assuming a number of roles. This is at once the weakness and strength of pastoral counseling. The pastor can draw resources from other parts of the congregation, but must avoid a conflict of interest with the partners. Disengagement requires exiting the counseling relationship without disrupting other relationships within congregational life.

The Method in Brief

Successful pastoral counseling depends on a successful encounter stage, which aims to instill confidence that the pastor will be helpful and depends on accurate assessment of the major problems.

During engagement, a pattern is established and may be followed throughout the remainder of counseling.

- Listen for the problem. Pinpoint the present failure of partners to mutually value each other.
- Trace the problem to the past roots. This may involve a past male-female relationship but will usually involve a parent-child relationship.
- Pinpoint hurts and devaluing in the partners' home life while growing up.
- Help partners forgive their parents for the hurts of childhood, effecting a healing of memories.
- Help partners repent of bad patterns that developed early in life and renounce those patterns in the present marriage.
- Identify alternative patterns of treating the spouse—to value and avoid devaluing the spouse.
- Provide ways, beyond counseling, for partners to grow in their general Christian discipleship, practicing Christian valuing in a wider context.

Conditions of Counseling in Brief

Generally, there are three conditions under which pastoral counseling can take place. Only one spouse may attend counseling with the pastor. This is usually the most common scenario, though it is probably the least desirable.

In a second scenario two Christian spouses attend marital counseling together. The shared source of major values between pastor and the couple gives this counseling the highest probability of success.

A third scenario would have both partners attending marital counseling; however, one of the spouses professes Christianity and the other does not. While there is still a good chance that the marriage might be helped, there are additional dangers of perceived alliances and violated expectations.

Overview

Let us return to our dance analogy. You may have danced for years. You know the steps and can negotiate the dance floor in a graceful if not elegant style. Yet you want to improve your performance, so you engage a dance instructor to teach you new dance styles and techniques. At first, you are shown an overview. Then, with a vision of strategy and method, you can easily study the details of the dance. Finally, after hours of practice, you can employ the strategy and method to negotiate the twists, turns, and obstacles you encounter in a dance.

Similarly, now you have an overview of Strategic Pastoral Marital Counseling: the strategy (building faith working through love), the stages (encounter, engagement, and disengagement), the method (move from present marriage to family of origin and then back to the present marriage), and the conditions of counseling. With that vision, you are ready, in subsequent chapters, to delve more deeply into each aspect of Strategic Pastoral Marital Counseling.

—

Part 2

Three Stages of Strategic Pastoral Counseling for Marriage Conflicts

$$3$$

Encounter Stage: Promoting a Healing Relationship

Without encounter, progress won't happen.

Christianity is a religion of relationships—among the Persons of the Trinity, between God and individuals, between God and the collective church, and among Christians. At the encounter stage, the pastor's primary goal is to establish a healing relationship with the couple or individual partner that will facilitate effective assessment and will provide a basis for counseling.

We will divide the encounter stage into two parts. First, we will offer guidelines for promoting a healing relationship with the couple (this chapter). Second, we will offer guidelines about what to assess (Chapter 4) and will begin the case study of Bonnie, which will be continued in Chapters 8 and 9.

Forming Good Pastoral Counseling Relationships

Being Aware of Established Roles

Pastors have previously established relationships with most people they counsel. In that regard, they have an advantage over a professional counselor who must form a relationship with a stranger. (Of course, sometimes pastors counsel strangers, and in those cases, must quickly form a healing relationship.) Having an ongoing relationship with a parishioner has its down-side, too. In any relationship a person's behavior quickly falls into patterns, called roles. Roles help people know how to act with each other but roles are hard to break out of when people must interact in a new context, such as counseling. The following roles can affect a pastor's counseling.

- The he-or-she-is-my-pastor role. People have strong ideas about what they can safely tell pastors.
- The I'm-their-pastor role. Many pastors are accustomed to being treated as spiritual giants and may try to act that role in counseling, which can quickly drive counselees away.
- The preacher role. The typical parishioner sees the pastor mostly as a preacher, which may affect the counselee's expectations of counseling. The counselee may expect the same type of counseling that he or she receives from a sermon. Or the pastor may move sermons to the counseling room, which is unacceptable to most counselees.
- The volunteer role. When a church volunteer (e.g., elder, Sunday school teacher) seeks counseling, the pastor may not want to give difficult counsel, which risks alienating and thus losing an essential volunteer.
- The influencer role. When a pastor counsels a member of the board of trustees or policy-setting committee that has responsibility to approve or disapprove some of the pastor's pet projects, the pastor may feel reluctant to confront the person.
- The friend role. When a pastor counsels a long-time friend and his or her spouse, the prospect that the friendship will

continue long after the counseling ends could keep the pastor from making necessary demands on the counselees.

There are two essential tasks in forming a good counseling relationship: structuring counseling and joining with the counselee (by creating a warm emotional atmosphere and promoting agreement on tasks and goals).

Structuring Counseling

Generally, experienced counselors have found that expectations can be dealt with most effectively by structuring the counseling at the onset. Structuring is explaining what the person can expect from counseling, and it may include these components:

- how long counseling might last
- the experience and training of the counselor
- some important beliefs of the counselor
- a brief description of the approach used in counseling
- a discussion of any complicating factors
- an expression of hope about the outcome of counseling, assuming the counselee is willing to work hard

In structuring, the pastor points the way ahead. As we stressed earlier, the pastor does not want simply to assume a professional counselor's role. However, there are valuable tried-and-true suggestions that the pastor can easily adapt in counseling. If a pastor structures the interviews using these suggestions, the conversation might proceed as follows:

Pastor Bob: Before we get started, I wanted to be sure that we understand what we were about in counseling. I have found that we will accomplish the most if we confine our counseling to a brief period of time, usually no more than meeting weekly for five weeks. As a pastor, I would probably be out of my depth if we met for long-term counseling. If we haven't made substantial progress in five weeks, you should con-

sider getting help from a professional Christian
counselor. How does that sound?

Patricia: Well, Pastor Bob, we've been having trouble
for so long. Do you really think . . . ?

Roger: Pastor Bob, both Patricia and I are worried that
we can't accomplish much in only five weeks.

Pastor Bob: That may be true. I've counseled couples
for over 20 years and not all of them could solve
their problems in five weeks. I have seen God do
amazing things when both husband and wife really
wanted to work out their problems and were eager
to listen to God. From what I know about you both,
you have a heart for pleasing God. I believe that if
you work hard and if you maintain that sincere
desire to see God work in your life, then you can
make some progress.

Roger: Thanks. We'll do our best. But we've allowed
our tensions and anxieties to get to each other for
years. I hope we can do something.

Pastor Bob: As I said, we'll see. One potential hurdle
that we may have to overcome is the long relationship we have with each other. Even though we've
known each other for eight years, I've never counseled either of you. It'll be a new relationship for
both of us. Sometimes in counseling I might ask you
to do things that will be difficult for you. I might
seem to be siding with the other person against you.
I hope you know that I value both of you as friends.
Even though I have spent more time socially with
Roger than with you, Patricia, I will try to be fair
with both of you. I want to help you work out your
conflicts. That may mean being a little rough on
each of you at times. I hope you'll understand counseling as an expression of my love for you both. I
believe that God brought you to this congregation
and established a relationship between us for a purpose. I think we can confidently build on that rela-

tionship and on our faith in Jesus to help you deal
with some of these difficulties.

Structuring is necessary for effective counseling. It can help
shape realistic expectations for counseling and prevent some of
the potentially harmful effects of previously established relationships.

"Joining" the Couple in Marriage Counseling

How can the pastor move from the ongoing pastoral relationship into the pastoral counseling relationship? How does the pastor "join" the couple or individual for marital counseling?

Joining the couple means being accepted by the couple as someone who can help them work on their marriage. You might think
that when a couple requests counseling they are expressing a willingness to join with you. That is not always the case. People request
counseling for many reasons, some noble and others not so noble.
Some people are motivated by guilt, coerced by a spouse, advised
by an attorney, or mandated by a court. Their motivation to work
on their marriage is questionable. Occasionally, they are more motivated to resist the counseling than to change their behavior. The
pastor's initial job, then, is to establish a relationship that will per-
mit pastor and couple to collaborate on solving marital difficulties
and helping the partners build their faith.

Joining is an attitude you create with the couple, not a set of
techniques you perform. Joining is an attitude of mutual respect.
It involves a sense of sharing an adventure together. You are a guide;
they are participants in a hunt for wild animals. You are a coach;
they are a championship team in quest of the national championship, sometimes against desperate odds. You join the couple not
as an equal but as an equally essential member in pursuit of a heroic
quest.

To join with counselees, you must create positive expectations,
demonstrate your competence at carrying out your tasks, depend
on the partners to carry out their tasks competently, and thus build
cooperation.

Structuring counseling gives counselees a sense of what will happen in counseling and creates the foundation of joining with them. Joining—what professional counselors call creating a working alliance (Bordin 1979)—includes both the positive emotional connection between you and the partners and agreement on the tasks and goals of counseling.

Create a Positive Emotional Connection. Your strategy for counseling should have at its core that you value the counselee. There are some ways that reliably convey such an attitude.

- Use positive relationship skills such as active listening, validating, and empathizing with each person. Do not play favorites.
- Attend to feelings. When people believe something to be important, they *feel* strongly about it. Try to uncover strong feelings, especially unexpressed positive feelings that may have lain dormant during a period of conflict. Even "negative" feelings should not be denied because they provide a strong motivation to change.
- Attend to each person's description of the problem. Do not belittle it. Each spouse views the relationship from his or her perspective, which seems accurate to the spouse (but not to the partner). You hope to forge a common perception of the relationship—one that differs from either partner's and will allow the partners to love each other more and to focus on problems less.
- Acknowledge the couple's courage in seeking help in a difficult and threatening area. It is not easy to admit to a pastor that the couple's marriage falls short. The partners are to be admired for being willing to expose their difficulties when so many couples hide the difficulties until divorce is inevitable.
- Avoid "teaching" the couple about what you think to be the cause of their difficulties before they have provided ample evidence to support your conceptualization. Strategic Pastoral Marital Counseling views the basic problem as failure to love (i.e., value) the spouse. As partners tell their stories and interact, you will see ample evidence of this. Rather than immedi-

ately diagnosing this problem, allow the partners to tell their stories. Show interest, inquire about their failures to value each other, express empathy. This conveys that you value them. When you summarize your assessment by pointing out their failures to love, they will be ready to hear and accept your view of the problem.

- Enhance similarities between yourself and the counselees. Generally, people feel closer to people with whom they identify and feel similar to. When given the chance, emphasize how you are like the partners, not how you differ from them.

Promote Agreement on Tasks and Goals. To elicit agreement on the tasks and goals of counseling, follow these guidelines:

- Provide information about counseling
- Tell the counselees how they will benefit from counseling
- Assign tasks and negotiate goals with respect for the counselees

What information should be given about counseling? In two independent reviews, Orlinsky and Howard (1986) and Beutler, Crago, and Arizmendi (1986) found that orienting clients as to what to expect in therapy prior to their counseling will improve outcome. You may provide the information in many ways, including discussion, written descriptions of counseling, audiotapes, or videotapes (see Table 3.1 for some suggested information). The companion book to this volume, *Value Your Mate,* will also tell counselees what to expect in counseling. These media allow counselees to consider what counseling will be like without using in-session time.

Educate the couple about how they can benefit from counseling. Such recommendations might include encouraging partners to work at counseling, to persevere with counseling through good times and bad, to focus on their own change rather than on their spouse's deficiencies, to pray for each other, and to use the companion book we have provided for couples.

Review of How to Establish the Healing Relationship

Promoting healing relationships can be enhanced by following several steps. First, motivate people so you are sure they know they need to change and cannot solve their problems by maintaining the current course. Second, get people to think along with you, involving them in the thinking process by using their own information to conceptualize the problem and by allowing them to do as much of the thinking as possible. Third, make sure that people are clear about what needs to be done and how it should be done. Support attempts at change and follow up to see how people did and how they could improve in future attempts at change.

Some pastors seem to have the gift of establishing a healing relationship with their counselees without conscious effort. For most, though, effectiveness is increased through deliberate attention to structuring and joining and through an attitude of love.

Table 3.1

Guidelines for Benefiting from Counseling with a Pastor

- Couples who benefit from counseling are those who are involved in their counseling and do what is suggested.
- Tell yourself continually that divorce will not take away all of your distress; it merely substitutes other distress for the present.
- Adopt the attitude, "I have fallen out of love, and I can fall back in love."
- Change first; don't wait for your partner to change.
- The most important principle of change is this: "Jesus loves me even when I am unlovable. He thought I was valuable enough to die for. Because of that, I can love my spouse even if I don't feel loving toward him or her right now. I must show my partner that I value him or her in everything that I do. I must even be willing, like Jesus, to lay aside my rights, comforts, and desires at times to show how much I value my partner."
- Risk trying to change, even if you have tried previously and failed.
- Be patient; be willing to do things that are not comfortable to allow healing.

- Expect ups and downs in counseling. When the downs come, don't stop trying to change. When the first ups come, don't think the problem is solved. Keep working until valuing your partner becomes a habit.
- Don't quit just because you don't see quick progress.
- Don't expect your spouse to become perfect.
- Pray for yourself and your spouse; it is through prayer that God changes your spouse *and* you.

4

Engagement Stage:
Assessing the Problems

Effective counseling requires good assessment.

Marital problems are caused by failure to love. Yet we still must assess each couple carefully. We don't know exactly how particular partners fail to value each other, in which areas of the relationship failures in valuing occur, how the failures to value the partner depend on the history of the partners, and how to best help the couple build a better marriage.

Effective assessment depends on knowing where to look. Evaluate the following nine areas: Christianity, core vision of marriage, confession and forgiveness, closeness, communication, conflict resolution, cognition, covenant and commitment, and complicating factors. We will discuss each. At the end of this chapter, we begin the fictional case of "Bonnie," which shows how Strategic Pastoral Marital Counseling might be applied. We follow Bonnie through each stage of counseling, including the encounter stage (Chapter 8) and the disengagement stage (Chapter 9).

Christianity

Using Christian Values in Pastoral Counseling

While it is not fruitful to assume that every counselee will be a dedicated Christian, it can be assumed—because the person has sought help from a pastor—that the counselee will expect that the pastor's Christian values will be used in counseling. Many people today are fed up with the poverty of secularism. They feel a spiritual emptiness and come to a pastor hoping that his or her spiritual experience and perspective will provide a dimension that secular counseling cannot.

Although counselees anticipate and want a clear Christian perspective from the pastor, they are also part of the modern psychology-wise culture. As such they will not tolerate attempts to impose Christian values on them. Value imposition by the pastor depends on the counselee's perception. At one extreme, a pastor might impose values by insisting on one theology, understanding of Scripture, or view of a problem and by coercing a counselee to agree through threats of disapproval, criticism, or withdrawal of counseling. At the other extreme, some counselees may feel that the pastor is imposing his or her values at the mere mention of Christianity.

What to Assess

The Strategic Pastoral Marriage Counselor should assess several aspects of the counselees' Christianity.

- Assess the counselees' spiritual life. You must judge how to speak to the counselees in a way that is most likely to be heard and least likely to be perceived as coercive or judgmental. You must earn the right to be heard by creating a climate of trust and love.
- Assess how the counselees might react to talk about salvation, religiously oriented interventions, prayer, or discussions/suggestions of confession, repentance, and forgiveness. The pastor wants to be like Jesus, who met those whom he helped at their point of need, whether in restor-

ing sight, curing paralysis, or reasoning (with Nicodemus), and later moved beyond that area into the person's spiritual neediness.

- Assess each partner's Christian commitment and spiritual maturity.
- Assess partners' connectedness to other Christians, individually and within groups. Do the individuals have friends who are committed Christians? Do they participate within the church? Belong to a small group? Minister openly to the community? How much support do they have?
- Assess how the partners integrate God within their marriage and family life. Is their relationship to God observable? Is it private? Hypocritical?
- Assess counselees' understanding of marriage as a sacred versus a secular act. Is marriage seen as ordained and maintained by God, or is it something that individuals do apart from God?

The main purpose of assessing each of these aspects of Christian commitment is to determine how receptive each will be to God's pattern of dealing with marriage—faith working through love. While dealing with marital problems is the counselees' major concern, the pastor is equally or more concerned with the counselees' faith and obedience to God's ways.

The Core Vision of Marriage

Assess the Ideal and Actual Vision of Marriage

As people act, they manifest their vision of marriage. The core vision of the marriage consists of two parts: the ideal vision of marriage and the vision of the marriage as it is perceived actually to be. Each partner has a vision of himself or herself, the partner, and the relationship.

Much of the person's ideal vision is discernible from examining the family of origin of each spouse. Thus, much will be learned about the core vision of marriage in the second interview during which a family-of-origin and a marital history will be taken. People learn much about how they should and shouldn't behave within the family of origin.

Other aspects of the ideal vision of marriage are shaped by such experiences as previous relationships, reading, television, exposure to general culture, and sharing ideas about marriage with the spouse. The ideal vision is affected by the experiences the person has with the partner. Painful experiences have reduced the initial romance and may have affected the hope the person feels.

You might assess these aspects of the person's vision of the marriage by asking, "What do you think your marriage could be like under ideal circumstances? How would you act if everything were perfect?"

The differences between the perceived actual vision and the ideal vision may be investigated through questions such as, "How does your marriage differ from what you think it could be?" It is important to probe to discover specific ways that the perceived actual vision differs from the ideal vision.

Assess How Partners Have Tried to Improve the Marriage

Find out what partners have tried to do to make their relationship better. For example, you might ask, "You must have tried many times to achieve this goal, right? Tell me what you've tried so far to make your marriage better." This accomplishes three purposes. It underscores that the partners have not been able to solve the problem on their own, which makes them more receptive to God's intervention and to your suggestions; it helps prevent you from suggesting solutions that have already been tried unsuccessfully; and it allows you to uncover ways that the couple have tried to improve their marriage. Often such clues, when continued and perhaps expanded, can provide effective ways that the couple can solve their problems (de Shazer 1988) and opportunities for encouragement.

Confession and Forgiveness

The capacity to confess sins and failings and the willingness to forgive are essential to the longevity of any marriage, regardless of whether it is Christian. Hurts are inevitable in marriage. Without the capacity to forgive and to ask for forgiveness, the marriage will continually be plagued by pain, anger, distress, and resentment.

Early in counseling, assess the couple's capacity for confession and forgiveness by observing how each person describes the marital problems. Request that each partner describe only what he or she has done to contribute to the problem, *not* the partner's wrongs. For example, you might say, "Would each of you, in turn, tell how you have contributed to the stress in your relationship. Try to avoid talking about the other person's faults." Generally, despite this directive, each partner will blame the other. The tenacity with which the partners blame each other will give you an initial idea of the difficulty that unforgiveness is likely to be in counseling.

Closeness

Closeness is an outgrowth of the partners' core vision of marriage, which is an outgrowth of their Christian spirituality. Partners may value or devalue each other by the ways they treat closeness. Do the spouses value each other by desiring to remain in contact in spite of conflicts? Do they devalue each other by rejecting closeness?

Closeness is multidimensional. There are five types of intimacy: emotional, sexual, social, intellectual, and recreational (Schaefer and Olson 1981). Assess each.

Closeness is regulated by the way that people spend their time. Each activity promotes either intimacy, distance, or co-action. Intimate activities promote feelings of emotional connectedness. For example, enjoying sexual contact, discussing future plans, or reminiscing are intimate activities. Distancing activities can only be done alone. For instance, sleeping, reading, studying, taking a solitary hike, or working on a coin collection might be distancing activities. Co-active activities are done with another person but do not produce intimate feelings. Going to a movie, playing a sport, or discussing childrearing practices might be co-active.

Although the needs for intimacy, distance, and co-action are related to each other in that all activities added together total 24 hours in the day, they are partly independent of each other. For instance, a woman who spends most of her waking hours tending a baby may experience deficiencies in both intimacy and distance activities because she spends so much time co-acting with her baby. Thus, she feels like she never has intimate time with her husband or a minute to herself.

How people talk about their needs for intimacy, distance, and co-action is not always how they act.

A romantic notion of marriage holds that the spouse should meet the partner's entire need for intimacy. This is not practical and probably not desirable. Friends and co-workers may also meet needs for intimacy (except, of course, for sexual intimacy).

Closeness can be assessed early in the interview by determining how the partners spend their time and by asking directly about how each partner experiences emotional, sexual, social, intellectual, and recreational intimacy relative to what they would like to have. Pay special attention to emotional intimacy, which many couples consider the most important. How do partners show that they value each other in each type of intimacy? Do they devalue each other's needs for intimacy, distance, or co-action? Observe patterns of behavior and discern from the conversation whether other unobserved patterns are present.

Communication

Good and Not So Good Communication

Communication is the verbal or nonverbal exchange of information. People value or devalue each other through communication. Most troubled marriages are plagued by poor communication. However, even in good marriages, partners may sometimes have difficulty communicating.

Every communication has three aspects: what is said, how it is said, and what implications the communication has for the partners' relative power. For example, suppose that a husband is talking about the difficulties he has encountered at work that day. Suddenly, the wife interrupts, shouting that he never pays attention to her, that he always is self-centered and talks about his day at work upon arriving home, and that she has had it with such selfish behavior.

Most counselors would agree that this was not good communication by the wife. The wife's communication devalues her partner (because she feels devalued). If the wife can see how she is devaluing her husband through her communication, she may change her communication to value him more.

Focus on Only One of Three Aspects of Communication

The above message may be analyzed in terms of *what* is said. The wife does not acknowledge what her husband says, nor does she indicate that she understands him. Her lack of interest says that her agenda is more important than his, a message that devalues him.

The message may be analyzed in terms of *how* it is said. The wife's interruption conveys again that her speech is more important than her husband's. Further, her screaming tirade does not respect her husband. In both ways, she devalues him.

The message may be analyzed in terms of the implications for each spouse's *power*. This couple seems to have an ongoing power struggle. It is unclear how the power is actually apportioned. It may be—as the wife suggests—that she feels powerless and her communication is an attempt to gain power. On the other hand, it may be that she already has the lion's share of the power and wants more. The power struggle suggests that both are dissatisfied with the value each has for the other.

Usually you will favor one way of analyzing communication. Whatever way you use, communicate to the couple that each person is not valuing the other through this conversation.

Assess Leveling and Editing

Leveling is telling the partner whatever comes to mind regardless of the impact. Some people level too much. They lower the boom on the partner whenever they don't like the slightest thing, which conveys that they don't value the partner. Others level too little, which is called editing. Regardless of what happens, they don't share their thoughts and feelings with their partner. Thus, the partner may feel untrusted. Both too much leveling and too much editing do not value the partner. The biblical model is to speak the truth *in love* (Eph. 4:15).

Assess Expression of Emotion

Generally, troubled couples will express their feelings within the counseling session, especially their negative feelings. Most people edit more when speaking in front of their pastor than they do at home, but they still express anger. Watch how emotions are expressed and note when emotional expression devalues the partner or builds the partner up.

Don't allow the free expression of negative emotion within counseling. If you can't regulate the couple's expression of hurtful, negative emotions, they will be reluctant to continue counseling. The tightwire act for the counselor is to help the couple express negative emotions without hurting or devaluing each other and in a way that will convey a valuing of each other and will help the partners resolve their negative feelings. For example, you might say, "Hold on a second, Susan. If I were Curt, I'd be hurt by the way you shouted at him. I can tell that you're angry, but can you express your anger so that Curt can hear it?"

Conflict Management

Assess the Amount and Style of Arguing

All couples must resolve differences, but not all couples argue to resolve them. Arguing is unresolved, emotion-involving disagreement. Most troubled couples argue. (They might call it "discussing enthusiastically," but they never seem to reach agreement.)

Sometimes troubled couples give up hope of resolving the conflict and withdraw. They harbor resentment and anger within a shroud of hopelessness, but they never "argue." Their relationship exudes devaluing, and conflict becomes a stimulus to hurt and put down the partner.

The best way to assess the couple's usual style of conflict resolution is to observe them as they discuss some issue about which they have had long-term disagreement. It may even be useful to audiotape the conversation (with the couple's permission, of course) so that strengths and weaknesses of their conflict style and ways that they value and devalue each other can later be pointed out to them.

Assess the Involvement in a Power Struggle

Often, troubled couples become trapped in ineffective attempts to resolve differences. They insist on a position that allows no room for other solutions. For example, Jules might say, "Listen, women always do the household chores, they've always done them, and it doesn't seem like that's debatable."

People really desire to have their interests met, not just get acquiescence to their position. When they insist that there is only one way to meet those interests, however, they effectively shut out any solution except their own. Generally, such insistence is at the center of a power struggle. A power struggle is, by definition, a struggle of relative value within the relationship. If you detect the presence of a power struggle, look for ways that partners are devaluing each other.

Assess the Areas of Conflict

Areas of conflict are important more for your information than for their use in resolving conflicts. Common areas of disagreement in marriage are sex, money, childrearing, chores, in-laws, personal habits, and use of time. Pastors may identify areas of conflict rapidly by using a powergram (Stuart 1980) or simply by asking.

It is important not to become a mediator whose sole function is to resolve conflicts for the couple. Rather, help the couple learn how to resolve conflicts themselves without having to depend on you as their referee. For instance, if one partner says, "What do you think about it, pastor?" you might say, "I could tell you my opinion, but the important point is that the two of you need to learn how to resolve these issues, not just get a quick-fix answer from me."

Assess Use of Two Stages of Problem-Solving

There are two steps to resolving differences: defining and solving the problem. Most troubled couples cannot agree on exactly what the problem is so almost no effort is made to solve problems. Assess the degree to which partners cannot agree on the problems they are trying to solve. Further, assess any efforts at arriving at solutions.

Assess Unproductive Disagreement Strategies

Troubled couples disagree in many unproductive ways (see Gottman 1979). For example, they may cross-complain. Each person states his or her complaints without acknowledging the partner's and without attempting to deal with the complaints. (Husband: "I'm angry with you because you smeared toothpaste on my pillow and I got it in my ear." Wife: "I'm frustrated because your beard tickles me." Husband: "Well, I'm furious because you shaved the left side of my face while I was asleep last night.") Or they may get sidetracked by discussing how they are arguing instead of trying to solve the problem. (Husband: "Don't raise your voice at me." Wife: "I'll raise my voice any time I want; it's my voice.") Or they might be unwilling to compromise. (Husband: "That's the way it is. I refuse to talk about it any longer. I'm going to sleep.") Or they may state their dissatisfaction vaguely. (Wife: "I'm upset." Husband: "About what?" Wife: "Things you're doing.") Or they may try to uncover who started the argument in the mistaken belief that if they discover who started it, it will magically disappear. (Husband: "You started it by raising your voice." Wife: "Yeah, but you upset me yesterday, so I was justified in raising my voice." Husband: "Yeah, but you lied to me once on a date, so I . . . " Wife: "Yeah, but Adam said to Eve . . . ") Each problematic communication devalues the spouse and fosters resentment, retaliation, and reciprocal devaluing.

Conflict resolution is complex. During an argument, emotion is high, and the pastor usually wants to remove the emotion and restore the couple to bliss. During assessment, your task is difficult. You must allow the couple to disagree enough to diagnose their problems accurately and detect ways they devalue each other, but you must be able to control their hostilities enough so that they will have confidence that you will provide a safe environment for them to work on their marriage. Assessing conflict resolution is thus one of the most challenging and yet crucial aspects of helping the troubled marriage.

Cognition

Cognition is mental activity—thinking and imagining. In psychological jargon, cognitions are specific thoughts, mental processes, and images. Among those cognitions most affected by a troubled marriage are assumptions, expectations, perceptions, attributions of cause, memories, self-verbalizations, and self-instructions. The relations among the various cognitions are complex. Generally, assumptions about the world and the self lead to expectations about what will occur. Assumptions and expectations affect how events are perceived. Perceptions, in relation to assumptions and expectations, determine the way we attribute cause of events. Perceptions are stored as memories. We then think words to ourselves—self-verbalize or self-instruct—to tell ourselves what to do and what not to do.

Assumptions about a relationship are based on the partners' experiences with their families of origin, their past experiences with other date or marital partners, and their experience with the current partner. Assumptions are based on perceptions that are encoded as memories.

Expectations rule what partners look for in a relationship and often become self-fulfilling prophecies.

Perceptions depend on what occurs (and what doesn't occur) in a relationship filtered through a lens of what is assumed and expected in the relationship. We usually assume our perception is accurate, but it may not be similar to someone else's perception of the same event. Marriage partners in conflict often disagree about the "true" problem. Each partner's perception is valid given his or her frame of mind, yet each perception is not the whole story.

When people experience stress, they try to explain what is happening. An explanation of cause is called an *attribution*. Their explanations—to themselves and to others—can help or hinder the solution of their problems.

Memories are parts of the mental sphere that are relatively enduring. Generally, assumptions, expectations, perceptions, and attributions of cause are memories. As with physical structures, memories are relatively permanent but are not impervious to change. Modification of memories is one of the implicit goals of marriage counseling, regardless of whether it is specifically focused on.

Partners base assumptions, expectations, perceptions, and attributions of cause on their memories of past events. Research suggests that each time we remember a past event we have the potential to reshape the memory of it—if the emotional environment is different than it was previously. Memories are more like plants grown from seed than videotapes. Each time a new seed is planted, the plant looks slightly different from the plant of the previous generation. So do memories. Memories get more negative in a negative environment but can be healed in a healing environment. This suggests that memories may be actually reshaped by positive experiences in the marriage, in counseling, or through God's intervention.

Self-verbalizations are thoughts people utter as their "stream of consciousness." Many times, people within a troubled relationship will self-verbalize a steady stream of negatives, keeping themselves in a distressed or angry mood and preventing themselves from changing.

Self-instructions are thoughts about how to accomplish goals. For example, the dissatisfied husband might think, *I'm going to try to keep a positive attitude, even if she complains continually about how much work Christmas is*. Partners describe to themselves what to do to change their relationship. Often the self-instructions are not likely to result in positive changes in the relationship. For instance, the wife might think, *He's not going to make me pay more attention to him just because he complains about working hard. I work hard too, and I'm going to complain as much as he does.* Self-instructions need examination. They reveal difficulties in reaching goals and often suggest unverbalized goals that prevent spouses from making positive changes in their marriage.

You can assess each partner's cognitions by listening to how each partner talks about the problems.

Covenant and Commitment

Christian marriage, mirroring Christ's eternal commitment to Christians, has traditionally been based on covenant. Covenant often involves self-sacrifice and always involves treating the person with whom the covenant is formed as equally (or more) important as the self. In biblical days, covenant meant an agreement lasting until the death of *both* parties. Sometimes one member of a covenant would die and the surviving member might care for the partner's offspring. A covenant usually was ratified through the shedding of blood. In ancient biblical times, animals were slain. In other cultures, participants cut themselves and dropped blood into a common cup, after which it was mixed with wine or other liquid and then drunk. In Native American cultures, "blood brothers" cut their arms or hands and let their blood flow together for a time. Such blood covenants were lifelong commitments.

In recent years, covenant has been used to mean simply an agreement that one hopes to keep. The consequences of covenant-breaking (loss of self-respect and respect for others, loss of honor, loss of face, and cause of eternal shame) have been lost in our modern casual use of the word "covenant."

Assess partners' commitment to each other as a lifelong marital commitment and their commitment to work hard to improve their relationship. We began examining the relationship by assessing the partners' commitment to Christianity. Their sense of commitment to the marriage complements their religious commitment.

Complicating Factors

Many things may interfere with work on marriage problems. Especially common is one spouse's severe psychological problems. Often this may involve drug or alcohol abuse, deep depression or other psychological difficulty, childrearing problems, physical debilitation or illness, or unemployment.

Another common problem is an ongoing or an unforgiven affair. A sexual affair is fundamentally a violation of trust that strongly communicates that the partner having the affair does not value his or her partner to meet the most intimate need in their marriage. If marital counseling is to have any chance of success, affairs must be terminated immediately. No marriage can compete with an affair. An affair is intimacy without responsibility, benefit without cost. When a person compares his or her happiness with the affair to life in a marriage, the affair will win because it is free intimacy.

Another complicating factor is a sense of whether the difficulties are openly presented or are hidden. When partners are reluctant to discuss their difficulties because they are ashamed of their behavior, counseling can be more complicated.

Summary of Our Assessment

Marriage is like a bicycle wheel. If the wheel is well balanced and the parts work together, then progress can be made and the ride is smooth. However, if the wheel develops problems, then the ride is bumpy and effortful, and the bicycle soon falls apart, injuring the riders.

The core vision of marriage is like the axle of the wheel. If the axle is faulty, warped, or fouled by sand, the wheel cannot function well.

Confession and forgiveness represent the inner rim, which fits around the axle and contains the ball bearings that lubricate the wheel. Confession and forgiveness are central to marriage because they hook into every aspect of it.

Closeness, communication, conflict resolution, cognition, and complicating factors are the spokes of the wheel. Difficulties in these areas arise because of stress in either the axle, inner rim, outer rim, or tire. If a damaged spoke is not repaired, the entire wheel may eventually become unusable. Mostly, though, problems with the spokes are manifestations of a deeper problem.

Christianity is the outer rim that holds the spokes in place, supports the tire, and allows the wheel to turn about the axle. If bumps and warped spots in the outer wheel are not repaired, the spokes become misaligned and the inner rim warped; the axle can even break.

Commitment is the tire that absorbs shocks and provides for a smooth ride. It rests on the rim of Christianity most comfortably and holds its shape when it fits snugly on the rim.

The frame of the bicycle holds the two wheels together so they can function toward a common end. The rider of the bicycle is God, who gives power to the bicycle to move it where he wants. Further, he is the one who can ultimately repair difficulties with the wheel.

In the encounter phase, you establish a healing relationship and assess the many areas of marriage. It might be difficult to remember all of the areas at first. To help you, we have supplied a worksheet, which you can photocopy and use to record your impressions about each couple (see Table 4.1).

Table 4.1
Assessment of Major Areas of the Marriage

Major Focus?	Male	Female
	Christianity	
	Core Vision	
	Confession and Forgiveness	
	Closeness	
	Communication	
	Conflict Management	
	Cognition	
	Covenant and Commitment	
	Coping Repertoire	
	Complicating Factors	

To understand more about the encounter stage, we describe "Bonnie," a fictional character who consults the fictional "Pastor Buck."

The Case of Bonnie

It's a long way from rural Georgia to the suburbs of Boston, thought Pastor Buck. *But the problems really haven't changed.* He looked at Bonnie, who huddled on the couch in his office. Bonnie was a beautiful woman of 37, short and thin with close-cropped wavy hair. Her eye makeup was running down her face with the tears that cascaded from her eyes as she talked about her marriage of 15 years with Walter. She dabbed at the black streaks on her cheeks and made apologetic sounds. Pastor Buck echoed her apologetic sounds, uncomfortable with her obvious embarrassment.

Bonnie's emotion had come soon after she began to describe her marriage. Their meeting had been set up to discuss Bonnie's two-year-old daughter, Cheryl. Buck explained that he was willing to meet with Bonnie up to five times, if necessary, to work on her problems with Cheryl. Shortly after Bonnie began to describe Cheryl's "tantrums," Buck asked how Walter dealt with Cheryl's problem. Bonnie burst into tears.

"Walter's having an affair. I'm sure of it," she said.

"Why do you think so?" asked Buck.

Bonnie sniffed. "He stays away at work all the time, and he gets up in the morning and rushes off. He goes in on Saturday, and he stays late. He's always been so laid back and unmotivated about his work. Now, he's 'at work' every time I turn around. He *must* be having an affair." She pounded a frail fist on the sofa as she said "must."

Pastor Buck had seen his share of affairs in his 44 years of ministry. It seemed as if affairs popped up, even in the church, whether in rural Georgia, where he had pastored a small church for 15 years, or in downtown Atlanta, where he had spent the next 29 years, or now in suburban Boston, where he was in his third month of ministry.

Buck nodded. "You sound as if you've been gathering evidence."

She looked up, and Buck smiled softly.

"No," she said. "I'm just so *puzzled*. It isn't like Walter, so I naturally assumed it was an affair. There's really not any *evidence* of an affair, just my suspicions."

"Umm. How has your marriage been—up until these suspicions, that is?"

"Our marriage has been fine. We've had some trouble with Cheryl. We didn't expect to have any children. We hadn't for all those years. Then, I got pregnant. It was a shock."

Bonnie put the wadded-up tissue in her purse that sat beside her on the sofa. "Cheryl seems to throw a tantrum every time I leave her. When I come to Bible study, she cries the whole time I'm gone. If Walter and I go out—which we hardly ever do—Cheryl cries when the baby sitter arrives and screams when we leave. But it's mostly when I'm alone with her and leave. When I leave her in the day care at the YMCA while I'm working out, she cries as soon as we enter the door and is usually crying when I pick her up."

"How long has this gone on?"

"It started about two months ago. Do you think it's normal separation anxiety for a two-year-old?"

"Well, I'm not sure. I'm not an expert, but it sounds more extreme than most children."

"I'm worried about her. She seems so normal except for those times. Of course, she clings a lot lately. It's a little aggravating."

"So when she seeks affection from you, it aggravates you?"

"That makes it sound as if I don't like her. I do. I love her. It's just that, well, I don't want to love her *too* much. You know what I mean?"

Pastor Buck shook his head. "Not exactly."

"I mean, what if there's a divorce? What if I've wrapped my whole life up in Cheryl? If there's a divorce, the judge would probably give Cheryl to Walter. He could care for her. I can't. I don't have any skills. I haven't worked and don't know how to do anything." She began to cry again.

After a while, Buck said, "You're pretty worried about the future of your marriage. Even though you said things are 'fine,' it sounds as if you're worrying about a divorce."

"Well, it's his fault. He's abandoned me. We don't ever communicate anymore, and if we do, we argue. We're hardly ever, uh, together, sexually, you know. I can't even get him to *talk* about anything but his business, much less love me. It's not right for him to do this to me. I have *needs*. He must be getting his needs met with someone else, you know."

Bonnie again made a fist, and her face flushed. "It's not supposed to be like this. I've been a good Christian since I was a teen. I've prayed, studied the Bible, gone to church, taught Sunday school. I always expected God to take care of his children, not hang them out to dry like this. If Walter is really having an affair, I don't think I can take it."

"You sound angry with God at the moment."

"I am. I know it isn't right, but I'm so *angry* I could just die."

Over the next hour, Buck explored the problems with Bonnie. As it neared the lunch hour, he wrapped up the meeting. "Bonnie, you've been very open and trusting with me this morning. I know that isn't easy, since you haven't known me long."

"But you're so easy to talk to."

"Still, you've shown a willingness to open up about your marriage that suggests to me that you really care about it. Let me see if I have the main threads of your worries. You seem to have several concerns, all of which may be tied together. Your main concerns seem to be Cheryl's crying whenever you leave her and the future of your marriage with Walter. You feel that you don't get much emotional or sexual intimacy from him, and you worry that he might be having an affair. You also don't talk together much and when you do, you argue. You express some sense of your own part in the marital tensions, but mostly you think Walter is to blame. Commitment is a major issue. You worry about Walter's commitment to you and you seem to be distancing yourself from both Walter and Cheryl in anticipation that the marriage might end and Cheryl would be taken by Walter. This may be contributing to the separation anxiety that Cheryl is feeling. She may not know why, but she may be sensing you pulling away from her. That threatens her, and she feels panicked whenever you leave her."

Bonnie was crying softly. Buck paused, then asked how that sounded.

"It sounds as if you've known me for years." She sat, head down. "But it all seems so hopeless."

"I don't think it's hopeless, Bonnie. The Lord is a great healer, and you've already shown an openness to him, even though you feel angry with him right now."

"I'm glad to hear you say that it doesn't seem hopeless to you. That gives me some hope."

"Good. Still, there's a lot to find out. Do you think you can take this understanding home with you and examine its truthfulness in the coming week?"

"I guess so. What should I do?"

"I thought it might be helpful simply to pay attention to your relationship with Cheryl and see whether it might be possible that fear of losing you is causing her clinging. Also, examine yourself before God, and try to assess your commitment to Walter. See if you are unconsciously hedging your bets."

Bonnie wiped her tears with one hand. "Thanks, Pastor Buck. I know that's what I need."

5

Engagement Stage:
History and Healing

The engagement stage will have two primary foci: (1) to promote healing through examining the history of the relationship and the individuals' families of origin and attempting to affect a healing of memories where appropriate; and (2) to help the couple deal with troublesome areas of their current marriage. In this chapter, we address the first focus.

Healing Through History-Taking

History of the Relationship

Marital problems are not born full-grown. They develop through each spouse's repeated failures in valuing, repeated devaluing, and repeated efforts to obtain valuing from the partner.

Regardless of whether you are counseling one spouse or both together, begin history-taking by saying, "You have told me about quite a few problems in your marriage, but I suspect that those problems didn't always exist. They probably grew as your relationship developed. It would be helpful if you described your relationship history since you met. Then I can understand the context of your problems and what you can do to get over them."

Having counselees describe the history of their relationship puts the marriage problems in context for both you and the counselees. It helps the partners see how their failures in love mounted over time; thus, the myth that a solution should occur instantaneously is weakened (though not eliminated).

History-taking also gives counselees hope and increases their motivation to change. In recounting the history of the relationship, people describe the good times in their marriage as well as the bad times. Pay at least as much attention to those good times as you do to the problems. By attending to the good times, you remind the partners that there are parts of the marriage that they would like to recapture.

During history-taking, you also help strengthen the conceptualization that marital problems are due to failures in love by attending to specific failures and demonstrations of love. You want counselees to see that a positive marriage embodies love and a troubled marriage fails to demonstrate mutual love.

To promote such a conceptualization of marriage, don't listen passively to the history. When a counselee describes a good time in his or her marriage, reflect back such phrases as, "During that period, it seems that you felt important to your spouse," or "At that time, you sensed that he (or she) cared for you," or "When he did that, you felt valued." After you have made such reflections several times, you can respond to other descriptions of good times by simply asking, "How did you feel about that?" They will usually answer that they felt valued.

Also during the history, you might respond to descriptions of the bad times in the marriage by reflecting how the counselee did not feel valued (important, cared for, etc.). At the end of the relationship history, say, "As you related the history of your relationship, I noticed that a pattern might be evident. It seemed that when you felt valued, the marriage went well, but that when you felt devalued or felt that your partner did not think you were important, then the marriage was more troubled. Is that the conclusion you draw?"

Helping the counselee draw such conclusions will prepare him or her for understanding the task of counseling as trying to love and therefore value the partner more than is currently evident.

History of the Families of Origin

After the counselees have described their history and you have concluded that failures in love have caused relationship problems, observe that those failures in love probably were learned when the counselees were young. Ask counselees to recount the history of their families of origin. Say, "You each have described ways that you put the other down, ways that you hurt each other, ways that you do not try to encourage and build up each other. Usually, such patterns were learned from your parents. Do you see any evidence of this in your families of origin?"

You are especially interested in determining two things. First, how did each counselee's mother and father treat each other? By finding out such information, you can discover much of the counselees' core visions of marriage. What marriage is hoped to be often depends on trying to duplicate or avoid parental patterns.

Second, how did each of the counselee's parents treat the counselee? Say, "How would you describe your relationship with each parent in a few words?" The opposite sex parent usually provides a model of how the person's partner should or should not behave within the marriage, but the same sex parent teaches how to respond to a spouse. Additionally, the same sex parent usually builds important patterns of rejection or acceptance in the counselee by the way the parent treated the counselee.

Rather than attempt to obtain a chronological history of the family of origin, elicit a description of a few critical events embodying ways that parents devalued or failed to value each other or the counselee. If such critical memories can be healed, the counselee can often be freed from bondage to them.

The final part of taking a history of the families of origin is to effect a healing of memories when appropriate. Often people in troubled marriages have been deeply hurt as children. They bring those patterns of hurt and response to hurt to their own marriage. The problems, while understandable and sometimes even appropriate within the family of origin, are not helpful for the current marriage, because the spouse *always* differs in important ways from the opposite sex parent.

Counselees need to be led to conclude that there are important differences between their relationships with the opposite sex parent and with the current spouse. If they can't see the differences, help them.

Healing Memories

You might want to pray with the person for the Lord to heal the hurtful memories of childhood. Memories are continually reconstructed as we gain different perspectives on a past event. The Lord can enter into the memories to change them by giving new perspective, promoting forgiveness, or simply taking away the emotional distress (see Seamands 1985).

There are many ways to help facilitate the healing of memories. Generally, you will help the counselee prepare for God's intervention, receive God's intervention, and move beyond God's intervention, applying the changes in his or her life.

Helping the Counselee Prepare for God's Intervention

Prayer by pastor and counselee helps the counselee be receptive to the intervention of the Holy Spirit in healing. God can sovereignly heal memories. We need to keep Jesus' example in mind during this time of preparation; his methods differed remarkably from person to person. God is creative. He is not bound by a single method.

The counselee must seek God's healing, but even more important, the counselee must seek God and be receptive to his will. This requires that the counselee acknowledge his or her neediness before God. The counselee affirms that only God can truly fill human needs and that, in particular, only God can truly meet the counselee's specific needs. Usually, such an affirmation will lead to praise of and thanksgiving to God by pastor and counselee.

This is not a method by which we force God into healing. It is not a required sequence of emotional or verbal experiences that the counselee must show. It is a progression of attitudes that makes the counselee receptive to the work of the Holy Spirit.

Helping the Counselee Receive God's Intervention

To help promote a healing of memories, the pastor guides the counselee so that he or she experiences the memory differently. Generally, this means that Jesus will be brought into the center of the memory. Some pastors have the counselee reconstruct one of the critical hurtful events in imagination. The pastor might instruct the counselee to imagine the event privately, or the pastor might narrate the scene and have the counselee imagine the memory as it is narrated. If narration is used, the scene should be consistent with the way the person described it during history-taking.

Alternatively, the pastor or counselee may simply pray for the people involved in the memory, bringing Jesus' role as redeemer from sin to bear on the memory. The counselee may pray to understand the people, forgive (where needed), or accept the past as part of God's plan. The focus of the prayer will differ for counselees with different needs.

Helping the Counselee Apply God's Intervention

Sometimes healing occurs quickly, sometimes slowly. Once God has intervened, the person will never be the same. Yet he or she may prevent total healing.

To use an analogy, assume that many years ago a person broke a hand. The broken hand was set, then immobilized for healing. Healing took place under the skin where it was not visible. When the hand was later released from immobilization, the muscles were atrophied, the hand weak, tender, and vulnerable. The person's tendency is to protect the hand, to use it only when necessary and to favor the hand. The protectiveness of the person is paradoxically the worst thing that could be done to complete the restoration of the hand to normality. Restoration requires use, exercise, and stress. In short, because X-rays are not available to this previously injured person, it requires *faith* that healing has taken place.

Analogously, healing of memories occurs where an X-ray cannot reveal God's healing work. It requires faith to accept God's healing of memories. Even if the memories have been healed—as in the analogy of the broken hand—the person must go beyond the mere healing of memories to be restored to full health. The person must behave without fear that he or she will reinjure himself or herself; must ignore the tenderness of the affected area but not place so much strain on it that it is reinjured; and must accept the need to use the affected part, to exercise it, and to intentionally expose it to some stress.

Once hurtful memories are confessed and healed, the person must stop behaving as if those memories still have hold of his or her life. The person must love others as a new creation. That intention and its manifestation within the marriage relationship will restore the person to full health.

Help Change Major Areas of the Marriage

In the first counseling session, you form a good working relationship and assess problems. In the second session, you listen to the counselees' histories and conceptualize them in terms of successes and failures of faith acting through love.

In the third session, you explore the problems in the area that is most troublesome for the couple. In the fourth session, you help plan what might be done to change their interactions within the troublesome area. In the fifth session, you help plan ways that change can be maintained. In each of the following three chapters, we will discuss common problem areas that you may address in these final three counseling sessions. In each area, we note ways that couples do not value each other and how to help them value each other more.

6

Engagement Stage:
The Christian Core

The Christian core of marriage involves the partners' Christian beliefs and values, their core vision of marriage, and their propensity to confess their wrongdoings and to forgive each other.

Christian Beliefs and Values

Strategic Pastoral Counseling deals with Christian beliefs and values within the context of solving marital problems. We discuss the goal of Strategic Pastoral Marital Counseling, describe concerns about counseling both Christian and non-Christian counselees, and provide guidelines on dealing with difficult theological questions.

The Goal of Strategic Pastoral Marital Counseling

Strategic Pastoral Marital Counseling helps develop more mature Christians through helping them solve their marital problems. With non-Christians, it is aimed at providing a Christ-centered approach to solving marital problems that will, we hope, lead the person closer to embracing the Lord.

The pastor must show how Christian discipleship applies to the marriage. Often, people who seem to be mature Christians in the church and the world do not live out their discipleship at home.

Counseling Christians and Non-Christians

Some couples come to counseling "unequally yoked"—with one spouse openly or covertly rejecting Christian truth. In these situations, it is helpful to approach Christians somewhat differently from non-Christians.

Counseling Christians. Goldsmith and Hansen (1991) have characterized a person's values as a stronghold surrounded by a marsh, which is located within a hostile forest. The stronghold represents the person's strongly held core values. The stronghold is surrounded by a marsh of uncertain footing—here solid, there treacherous. The marsh represents values that are less strongly held. The marsh is surrounded by a hostile forest. The forest represents rejected values.

In crisis, people rarely experience a complete change in their stronghold values or their forest values. Crisis attacks the marsh. Some of the vulnerable core values near the marsh-stronghold border may be sucked into the marsh, or some marsh values may wash up onto the stronghold and become core values. Some of the vulnerable rejected values near the marsh-forest border may also be eroded, becoming less strongly rejected, or alternatively some marsh values may move to the strongly rejected category. Crisis is a time of danger and opportunity.

Viewing values this way implies that the pastor should first bolster endangered Christian values through support and reassurance. Research on stress and religion (Mayton 1989) reveals that when bad things happen directly to a person, he or she often experiences a lessening of faith, but when bad things happen to a closely loved one, faith is often strengthened. Because marriage difficulties happen directly to the person, faith may be vulnerable.

On the other hand, marital problems straddle the boundary, also happening to the spouse (a loved one, at least at some time). Many people, especially Christians who have focused for years on self-sacrifice for other people, may view marital difficulties as a stimulus to turn to the Lord. Remain sensitive to how your counselee responds to marital difficulties.

Besides reassurance and support, you can help strengthen faith by calling attention to things learned through the difficult experiences. Be warned, though. A steady stream of positives from the pastor will usually be perceived as insensitivity to the couple's pain. Rather than strengthen faith, a Pollyanna focus will weaken faith. Instead, convey the biblical truth of God's good news that he is with us in our suffering while you avoid platitudes. Glib proof-texting, positive thinking, name-it-claim-it advice, and the well-meaning citation of well-known verses are usually counter-productive. If you intend to quote a well-known verse to a troubled Christian spouse, pause first and ask the person this question: "If you were going to give an excellent Bible verse for someone in your situation to meditate on, what would it be?" Most of the time, the person will quote the verse (or another good one that you wish you'd thought of) and you won't need to do it.

On the other hand, if you find that the urge to quote a well-known verse is overpowering, say, "I know you know it, but sometimes it's helpful to remind yourself of the eternal truths of Scripture (Rom. 8:28; Rom. 5:1; James 1:2–4; and others) . . . " Your preface acknowledges that you respect the person's knowledge and that you are not trying insensitively to apply a band-aid to what the person considers a major wound. You avoid the faith-without-works trap (see James 2:14–17). Rather than provide only the verbal veneer of faith, you show faith working through love as you respect the person and stick with him or her in working out problems with the Lord's help.

Counseling Non-Christians. Your assessment of people's Christian beliefs and values determines how you help them build their faith. Is Christianity in their hostile forest? Is it in their marsh of uncertainty? Is it between marsh and stronghold?

As Christ's ambassador, you don't want to drive people farther from Christ. Assess whether your most dangerous mistake would be to be too bold, causing a potentially receptive person to dig in his or her heels to resist a "hard sell," or not bold enough, failing to witness to a person who was ready to hear more of the gospel. Spiritual discernment is the key to this assessment. Spiritual discernment does not mean abandoning the decision to intuition or momentary reaction. Nor does it mean waiting for a felt leading by God, although sometimes that happens. Spiritual discernment usually means prayerfully and thoughtfully considering how to deal with the person while remaining sensitive to the Holy Spirit.

In counseling the non-Christian, as in all your counseling, demonstrate faith working through love. Usually, your most effective witness to the non-Christian will not come through quoting Scripture (though that may be appropriate at times) but through sticking with the person throughout his or her pain and making it clear that your motivation for such loving persistence is because of Christ's love to you and through you.

Dealing with Tough Questions

Marital difficulties often raise difficult theological questions. People may ask, "How can these painful things happen to me? I've always been faithful, loved and served the Lord. So has my spouse. How could God allow this to happen to us?" The person is struggling with the apparent conflict between God's love and God's justice. God is love and he is just. There is no *correct* answer for the person in pain. Answers that satisfy when lives are running smoothly don't always work when problems hit. It is tempting immediately to provide a well-reasoned, articulate answer. While that may be the very thing that some people need, most people will be more receptive to your answer if you show that you understand the person's struggles before you offer an answer.

Other difficult questions are frequently faced in marital counseling:

- Under what circumstances should separation occur?
- What should the person do if spouse or child abuse is occurring?
- When is divorce permissible? Advisable?
- When is remarriage permissible? Advisable?

Sincere and studious Christian scholars disagree on the answers to these questions. Because the questions arise so frequently, you must familiarize yourself with the arguments on all sides of the issues and think out your theological position in each case.

It appears, though, that your style of dealing with the questions (more than the content of your answers) will have the biggest impact on the counselee. The counselee-pastor relationship can be strengthened if the following guidelines are followed.

- Take the counselee's questions and struggles seriously; respect his or her logic and understand the person before you answer.
- Be "gentle." Treat the counselee as someone whom you'll love and respect even if he or she decides differently from you.
- Make it clear that there are different answers offered by wise Christians. Having done that, gently offer your opinion and support it.
- Avoid giving a sermon. Keep your answers short. Observe the counselee carefully while you are talking to make sure that what you are saying is being received and that you are not wandering from the counselee's issues to your own.
- Don't let counseling get bogged down in discussing theology. Investigating Scripture and Christian principles is a vital part of pastoral counseling, but getting sidetracked from counseling into argument or Bible study isn't helpful.

We have emphasized the enormous responsibility of the pastor to "live Christianity" during the counseling. The pastor should continually model faith working through love. Problems are conceptualized and people are dealt with by faith working through love. Content of Christian beliefs and values is important, but people can only hear what is being said when the pastor's actions are consistent with the content.

It is an awesome responsibility for an all too fallible pastor to be called to live out faith acting through love. We can only live out God's principle for Christian living with his help, which we receive through vulnerability before God in prayer.

The Core Vision of Marriage

Have you ever looked through binoculars?

Although binoculars improve your vision by magnifying what you are looking at, they also restrict your vision. It's hard to get an accurate "big picture" when you are looking through binoculars.

Couples with marital difficulties are looking at their marriage through binoculars. Their vision of their marriage is focused on their problems and disappointments, which are magnified, and they overlook large portions of their marriage. As their counselor, you want them to form a different picture of their marriage. You want them to turn the binoculars around when looking at their problems; doing so will shrink, though not necessarily eliminate, the problems. You also want them to focus on a different part of their marriage—the ways they do and can love their partner by actively valuing and avoiding devaluing the partner.

We will now examine the core vision of marriage and describe some ways to help change it.

A Closer Look at the Core Vision of Marriage

There are three parts of a core vision of marriage. Imagine three overlapping circles, as pictured in Figure 6.1a. One circle is the way a person thinks the marriage actually is (the concept of actual marriage). A second circle is the way the marriage really is (true marriage). The third circle is the way a person thinks the marriage should be (the ideal concept of marriage).

In the perfect marriage (which doesn't exist), the three circles completely overlap (Figure 6.1b). In reality, no one can ever know the true marriage, and no one's concept of actual marriage is completely the same as the true marriage. Everyone looks at their marriage through binoculars.

When things are going well, people train the binoculars on the positive events and feelings (Figure 6.1c). The concept of the actual marriage may not be very close to the true marriage, but it is close to the ideal. However, when things aren't going well, people train the binoculars on negative events and feelings (Figure 6.1d). They

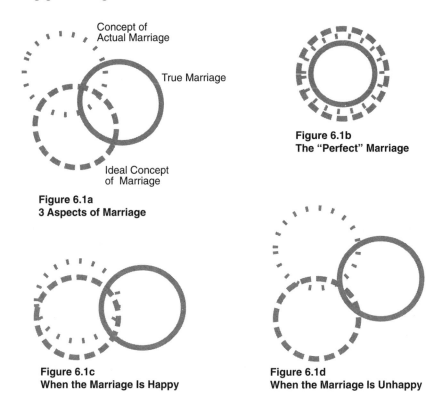

Figure 6.1a
3 Aspects of Marriage

Figure 6.1b
The "Perfect" Marriage

Figure 6.1c
When the Marriage Is Happy

Figure 6.1d
When the Marriage Is Unhappy

Figure 6.1

ignore and often distort their marital history, because they are looking mostly at the (limited) negative part of their marriage.

The third part of the core vision of marriage is the ideal concept of the marriage. This ideal is developed from a person's perception of his or her past experiences with family of origin, romantic encounters, previous dates or (perhaps) spouses, and ideals derived from popular culture.

As marital problems develop, people become more unhappy with their marriage. Like a ranger spotting smoke in the forest, the person looks through binoculars at the trouble spots and notices how far those spots are from the ideal. The person's concept of actual marriage is modified as increasing attention is paid to marital tensions and differences of the concept of actual marriage from the ideal concept of marriage. Past events are recalled and are actually transformed by the mind into more negative experiences than they really were. The concept of the actual marriage diverges farther from the ideal concept of marriage (again, see Figure 6.1d). Unhappiness is related to the amount of perceived difference between the concept of actual marriage and the ideal concept of marriage.

Helping Change the Core Vision of Marriage

You want to help the partners do three things: (1) remove unrealistic ideals and replace them with realistic, biblically consistent ideals; (2) move their concepts of actual marriage closer to their new, ideal concepts of marriage; and (3) move their true marriage closer to the new, more realistic ideal.

Replace unrealistic ideals with realistic, biblically consistent ideals. Throughout counseling, you will help most counselees develop a different ideal concept of marriage. First, describe biblically consistent patterns of marriage. Throughout this book, we have stressed the faith-working-through-love pattern. Marriage is a laboratory where people in close contact with each other can value each other despite the tensions between them. They must work constantly to prevent devaluing the other person, to confess their own failures at love, and to forgive the failures of their spouse. Your continual stress on faith working through love, confession and forgiveness, and covenant commitment will solidify a biblical concept of marriage.

Second, much of your attention during counseling will be to help people recognize and admit their unwillingness to take personal responsibility for their part in the marital problems. As they accept their own responsibility and imperfections, this should help them judge their partner less.

Third, as much as possible, couples should be involved with other couples in the life of the church. Try to pair the troubled couple with a couple who are functioning well and who can serve as good Christian models. Seeing other couples deal positively with marriage can affect a troubled couple's core vision of marriage. Couples might also be involved in a group composed of a variety of couples who are trying to live committed Christian lives and are willing to share their struggles with each other.

Move concepts of actual marriage closer to ideal concepts. Most troubled marriages have many positive aspects within their history and even their current experience, but like the person looking through binoculars, troubled partners can't see the positive. You need to help the couple focus their attention on the positive.

- During history-taking, spend at least as much time having couples describe their joys, reasons for marriage, and pleasant memories as you spend on their problems.
- When you summarize the status of the marriage at the end of assessment, talk at least as much about the marriage's strengths as about its problems.
- When spouses talk about intimacy, have them focus on successes as much as failures in intimacy.
- When couples communicate, point out instances of good communication and conflict management as well as instances of poor communication.
- Call attention to progress when couples work on their marriage.
- Interpret partners' efforts to change as evidence of their desire to improve their marriage and restore love.
- Treat people's motives toward each other as positive. They want to reestablish a loving marriage even when they hurt each other. Treat hurtfulness as a failure in carrying out their good intentions, not as evidence of lack of love.

Thus, throughout counseling, you continually help counselees adjust their concept of the actual marriage by attending to the positive events in the past and present relationship as well as to the negative. For partners in troubled marriages, the negatives arise spontaneously. You must help balance the books while showing the partners that you understand their pain.

Move the true marriage closer to the ideal. Although no one can ever truly know the "true marriage," you can help the couple move the true marriage closer to the ideal marriage. By having the partners actually behave more in line with the ideal, you affect the true marriage. To the extent that you help partners value each other more and devalue each other less, you move the marriage closer to the ideal. Further, you can help them speak the truth in love and live by faith working through love.

By shifting people's actual behavior, you help them change the true balance of negative and positive behaviors. It is imperative, then, that you help people act differently with each other, not just in the counseling session but between sessions. This suggests that you assign "homework." The companion book, *Value Your Mate*, gives concrete ideas for changing behavior. Assign counselees portions of the book to read and encourage them to employ the exercises that appeal to them.

Summary

People's marriages follow their vision. To affect the vision, you systematically help refocus their binoculars on faith acting through love. Help them see love when it actually occurs. Help them forgive failures in love and create new instances of love.

By the end of counseling, you will have made a small but significant difference in their vision, which will direct their path in the future. Don't be discouraged if you don't see giant changes in their direction. Large changes are rare in only five sessions of counseling. It is as if a man stands in Los Angeles and looks eastward. On the other side of the country, he sees Atlanta. If the man adjusts the direction of his gaze a mere two degrees of the compass, few people will notice the difference; yet the man now looks at Richmond, Virginia. Over a journey of many miles, he will end up in a vastly different city from Atlanta. That analogy describes your objective in pastoral counseling. Affect the core vision of marriage in a small but significant way, and the couple will end up in a vastly different place than they were headed at the beginning of counseling.

Confession and Forgiveness

Confession of failings in a marriage is essential for a healthy marriage. Confession is even more important for healing a troubled marriage because the hurts inflicted by both partners are usually more numerous and damaging than in a healthy marriage.

Equally essential is forgiveness of the spouse for hurting the partner. Forgiveness may be granted in response to the spouse's confession, in which case forgiveness usually should be oral and the offense should be never brought up again. Forgiveness may be granted unilaterally by a person who has been hurt, in which case forgiveness should be confessed to God but not usually to the spouse. Forgiving a spouse who has not asked for it nor confessed hurtfulness usually is interpreted as blame, which is antithetical to healing the marriage.

Occasionally, partners can't accept forgiveness. Partners who have sinned through a sexual affair, spouse abuse, or chronic drug or alcohol abuse often feel unworthy. For example, Howard had a drinking problem. For years, he got drunk publicly and embarrassed Katie. He was converted to Christianity and stopped drinking altogether. Howard confessed his sin repeatedly, and Katie, just as often, assured him that she forgave him. Howard, though, refused to accept the forgiveness, and within three months, he was drinking again. "Who could expect anything else from someone who is so worthless?" he asked.

Promoting Confession

Confession is seeing one's responsibility as a contributor to the marital problem, agreeing that one's actions are wrong, and desiring to change hurtful actions. You can help promote an attitude of confession, which is necessary for the healing of marital hurts.

Helping Individuals See Their Responsibility. In the abstract, almost every person will acknowledge that marital problems are partly the fault of both partners. Yet people do not live as if that truth permeated their hearts. It is natural for individuals to be self-focused, worrying about how others have hurt them and explaining their own hurtful actions as responses to hurts inflicted by their partners. But while natural, it won't help restore the marriage.

Throughout marriage counseling, promote acceptance of responsibility by requiring each person to talk for himself or herself, *not* for the partner. Preface comments to each partner by questions such as, "From your perspective, how do you see . . . ?" or "How did you experience . . . ?" When blaming statements are made, either point out that blame won't resolve differences or ignore the blame and focus on the individual's behavior. For instance, Monica might say, "Jason yelled at me, and I got so angry that I threw a bag of flour at him." The pastor might challenge the blaming statement gently by saying, "Monica, it sounds as if you are implying that somehow Jason's yelling *made* you throw the flour, as if you had no other way of dealing with the situation." Less confrontive would be, "Monica, when you got angry, you *chose* to throw flour to express your anger."

It is not helpful to accuse individuals of blaming their partner directly. For example, if the pastor had said to Monica, "You seem to be avoiding taking responsibility for your own actions of throwing the flour by blaming Jason," then Monica will probably become defensive. She may argue with the pastor, or logically insist that she wasn't trying to avoid responsibility, or outwardly accept the pastor's interpretation while inwardly harboring resentment. She will almost certainly feel devalued by the pastor—which is opposite to what the pastor is trying to teach (faith working through love)—and she will likely respond defensively.

This does not imply that the pastor should never confront counselees. Confrontation is sometimes necessary. Yet it is more easily accepted by counselees when they know you love and respect them than when they feel accused. Again, the loving, valuing relationship between pastor and counselee is the foundation on which successful counseling builds.

Helping Partners See That Their Actions Are Wrong. Partners come to see that their actions are wrong through prayer. When people stop talking at each other and stop being absorbed in their pain, and start praying, a melting often occurs, bringing them into voluntary confession of their sin. As they focus on God, not the spouse, they can stop defending and admit their mistakes, which in turn affects their relationship with each other. The Holy Spirit overcomes the flesh.

By promoting thoughtful reflection on behavior in light of Scripture, the pastor can bring the person in contact with scriptural truth, which can promote confession. In pastoral counseling, the pastor works in tandem with the Holy Spirit. The Holy Spirit convicts of sin, which frees the pastor from having to do so.

You can refer to times in your own life and marriage when you struggled with similar problems. This lessens defensiveness and promotes honesty.

You can also encourage thoughtful self-examination by looking carefully at the effects of communication on the partner.

Suppose Monica lashes out at Jason during counseling. "You're such an insensitive jerk sometimes. I just want to hit you."

Jason may retort angrily, "You never let your better judgment stop you from hitting me. Do you think that shows your sensitivity?"

The pastor should not allow such hurtfulness to continue. Nor does he. Pastor John holds up his hands. "Whoa! Just a minute! That kind of comment doesn't convey how you value each other, which is what you've been working on for weeks. Let's analyze this exchange. Monica, when you said Jason was an 'insensitive jerk,' what did you want to accomplish?"

"I got frustrated because he didn't acknowledge that I had been trying to keep the house cleaner. He came out with that snide comment about not inviting any of his business friends over, and it pushed my button."

Pastor John says, "You felt unappreciated and devalued, and you lashed out. What did you hope to accomplish?"

"I don't know. I didn't really think about *accomplishing* anything. I guess, though, I hoped to get him to notice that I'd been trying hard."

"How well did you succeed?"

"I didn't."

"John, when Monica called you an insensitive jerk, what effect did that have on you?"

"It made me mad."

"Merely mad? I might have felt hurt and put down in that situation as well as being angry."

"Yeah, I was hurt. I didn't mean to slight her. I didn't do it on purpose."

"But you see now that you did slight her?"

"Yeah." He turns to Monica. "I'm sorry."

Monica looks at Jason. "I'm sorry I called you a name. I was hurt."

Promoting a Desire to Change. Examining the effects of hurtful behavior, as in the case of Pastor John's counseling with Monica and Jason, can promote a desire to change, which Pastor John did in several ways. First, he showed that each person was not having the effect that he or she wanted to have. Rather, the effects of their communications were exactly opposite of what they desired. Second, he called attention to their goals, reminding them that they had been systematically working on valuing each other for several weeks. People respond well to clear goals. Third, Pastor John did not insist that the partners admit their wrongdoing. Rather, he led them through a consideration of their behavior and they spontaneously confessed their wrongdoing and expressed a willingness to change.

Promoting Forgiveness

Like confession, forgiveness can be stimulated as people consider their actions in prayer and in light of Scripture. You can discuss forgiveness with the partners, using the full range of pastoral methods of promoting forgiveness. For example, you might discuss the need to forgive by talking about the Lord's Prayer (Matt. 6:12) or the need to continually and persistently forgive by discussing Matthew 18:21–35.

The early part of counseling involves recounting family-of-origin histories, which will usually bring out an awareness of past hurtfulness within the family of origin that each partner perpetuates in their present marriage. As the pastor leads the couple through the healing of memories, forgiveness of parents is common. Often when a spouse hears the partner's past, he or she can become more tender, understanding, and forgiving.

In addition, as counseling nears its conclusion, the pastor may want to guide the couple through a forgiveness session, aimed at promoting forgiveness of other wrongs that were uncovered throughout counseling. Worthington has described the session in some detail in *Marriage Counseling* (Worthington 1989; see also Worthington 1990, 1991) and in an article co-authored with Fred DiBlasio (1990). Briefly, the pastor prepares the couple the week before the forgiveness session by directing each partner to identify hurts that he or she wants to confess to the other person. The following week, partners take turns confessing actions they know to be wrong. They may ask for forgiveness, but are cautioned not to grant forgiveness if they do not feel like it. Generally, a forgiveness session stimulates spontaneous emotional forgiveness and genuine contrition. It is not the method of the forgiveness session that promotes forgiveness. Rather, the tenderness of the counselor in preparing the couple and the trust that has been rebuilt throughout counseling allow forgiveness to occur.

The pastor is not the judge, prosecutor, or defender of the counselee. The pastor is one who, with the Holy Spirit, walks alongside, providing courage to the partners to examine themselves and their behavior toward each other in light of God's character. The pastor values the counselee, regardless of the nature of the counselee's actions—which can include affairs, abuse, lack of forgiveness, spitefulness, bitterness, and all manner of sin. The pastor's valuing must permeate all of counseling if the pastor is to lead the counselee to adopt a posture of faith working through love, which will lead to confession and forgiveness.

7

Engagement Stage:
Four Essential Elements
of Marriage

Couples must learn to make faith working through love permeate the Christian core of marriage. Faith working through love is manifested daily in four essential elements: closeness, communication, conflict resolution, and cognition. These are the areas in which you will spend the majority of counseling.

Closeness

People struggle throughout their lives to balance individuality against intimacy. It shouldn't be surprising that marriage brings out those issues probably more than any other relationship.

As you assess a couple, you may determine that closeness is an area in which you need to intervene. In this section, we describe four interventions:

- Helping adjust closeness and priorities through changing time schedules.
- Helping regain intimacy by strategically using your office.

- Helping with the pursuer-distancer pattern.
- Helping with some sexual problems.

Adjust Time Schedules

People attempt to meet their needs for intimacy, co-action, and distance through apportioning their activities. Each activity has some impact on promoting intimacy, co-action, or distance. Generally, people choose a career, a mate, and leisure activities to obtain a level of intimacy, co-action, and distance that feels comfortable to them. For example, a man who desires little intimacy may marry a woman who also can tolerate little intimacy, choose a career such as sales, which allows him to co-act with others but does not require intimacy, and use his leisure time in solitary or co-active pursuits.

We use our time to meet our needs for intimacy, co-action, and distance. If a man feels that his wife demands too much intimacy, he can adjust his job or leisure activities to get less intimacy there. If a wife feels that her husband is not meeting her needs for intimacy, she can change jobs, friends, or leisure activities to meet her needs.

If you suggest that a couple modify their time schedules to meet unmet needs, you will encounter resistance. It is difficult to make changes, and changes must be made over time rather than all at once. Further, once changes are initiated, the effects may ripple through the relationship for months or years, necessitating other adjustments. If the couple perseveres, both partners' needs for intimacy, co-action, and distance may be satisfied. Changing time schedules is difficult and costly. Characterize a partner's willingness to make such modifications as indicating that the partner loves and values his or her spouse enough to change.

Use Physical Space in the Office

One family therapy technique developed by Minuchin (Minuchin and Fishman 1981) is particularly effective in dealing with issues of intimacy. The office is used as a metaphor for emotional closeness or distance. Employ this technique to help a couple see that they can build intimacy through discussing topics about which they both feel positively. (Worthington has demonstrated this technique, and others, in a videotape for training marriage counselors. The tape is available from him for $15 at Box 2018 VCU, Richmond, VA 23284-2018. He has also described the technique in a case study—see Worthington 1991.)

The partners are asked to imagine that the distance from one side of the office to the other represents points of maximum emotional separation. Couples stand apart at the distance that represents how emotionally close they feel at the present. After that, they stand at the distance that represents how close together emotionally they ideally would like to be. (Usually, they hug.) Finally, they stand at a distance that represents their best realistically achievable emotional closeness.

Partners then pull their chairs apart to the distance that they currently feel, after which they discuss a pleasant shared memory. When you sense that they are more emotionally connected than they were at the beginning of the discussion, have them move their chairs closer together to represent the intimacy they now feel. Ask each to speculate about why they feel emotionally more intimate as a couple. (Each is feeling valued by the partner.)

Repeat these discussions with other intimacy-producing topics, such as goals, dreams, or memories of a time when they were particularly close. At critical points in each discussion, partners move their chairs closer. With this exercise, you want to show them, in about 25 minutes, that they can get closer to each other by having discussions that show love to each other. At the end of the discussion, ask whether each person feels valued by the partner.

Break Up the Distancer-Pursuer Pattern

A common pattern of conflict over intimacy occurs when one spouse, usually the wife, demands more closeness than the husband feels he can provide. So he demands more distance. (Sometimes the pattern is reversed, but not often.)

At advanced stages, the pursuer may simply give up, erect an emotional barrier, and lob insults and criticisms over the barrier. "I've been hurt for years and won't make myself vulnerable again," she might whine. The distancer, after initially feeling free from the ever-present demands for intimacy, may attempt to revive the relationship, but encountering the barrage of insults and criticisms, he may erect his own barrier and commence his own hostilities.

The ironic part of the distancer-pursuer pattern, and the part that fuels the pattern at all stages, is that neither spouse wants a lot of intimacy. Both are comfortable with moderate intimacy. They merely have different ways of keeping the other safely distant. The pursuer pursues so strongly that she drives the distancer away. The distancer runs away, but not too far away. Neither partner feels valued by the other. In counseling, you want each to decide to will to value the other, even if each must change his or her strategy of distancing or pursuing.

To deal with a distancer-pursuer pattern, spend most of your time talking to the pursuer. Don't pursue the distancer. If you demand that the distancer be more intimate with his wife, he will likely respond to you as he does to his wife—running away (perhaps even terminating counseling). Your demands don't value his wishes, so he will be unlikely to learn love through his interaction with you. On the other hand, if you treat him with respect, valuing his wishes and allowing him to show his love through laying down some of his desires for his wife, then he will more likely learn Christian love.

The same is true for the emotional pursuer. Pay close attention to her. In the short run, by attending to the emotional pursuer, you meet some of her desire for attention and reduce some of the pressure on the distancer. Help the pursuer meet some of her needs for intimacy elsewhere (except for sexual intimacy, of course). Help her avoid criticizing her spouse, and help her value her husband. Restore the positive atmosphere of the relationship. As the wife takes pressure off the husband, the husband will probably feel more need for intimacy. Suggest (but don't order or demand) that he initiate some intimate activity that he thinks his wife would enjoy. Help her accept whatever intimacy is offered without criticizing or demanding more. As the partners change these deep-seated patterns of behavior, commend them for their willingness to value each other above their own needs.

Provide Information to Help with Sexual Problems

Sexual problems often occur within troubled marriages. Most of the time, they seem to be a result of other relationship difficulties that suggest failures in love and valuing, such as lack of emotional intimacy, poor communication, constant conflict, bitter blaming, and the like. They usually indicate a failure of partners to value the other person.

This is not always true, though. Sometimes marriages may be excellent, but partners may be ill-informed about maintaining a good sexual relationship; have faulty ideas about how to stimulate each other sexually; hold beliefs that are harmful such as "the male should know how to bring his wife to orgasm without her needing to tell him what feels good and what doesn't" or "the only good sex is simultaneous orgasm"; or disagree over acceptable sexual positions or behavior. Many such difficulties may be solved if you provide accurate information or good reading material. One source for your own reading is Joyce and Clifford Penner's *Counseling for Sexual Disorders* (1990).

We recommend not dealing with sexual issues with an individual counselee of the opposite gender. Refer such a counselee to your own spouse or to a talented and trained lay helper for information, or co-counsel with another counselor of the same gender as the counselee. Pastors are particularly vulnerable to sexual temptation (Shackelford 1989). In fact, in research by Berry (1991), over half of a sample of about 100 pastors reported some sexual contact with a parishioner at some time in his or her career.

Summary

When partners feel unloved primarily because they sense problems with closeness, help eliminate feelings of being devalued and restore a sense of mutual valuing. Often partners feel that their emotional intimacy has died. Only God can resurrect it, but like the physician who puts the cast on a broken arm to provide protection while God heals the arm, you can help partners straighten out the break in their intimacy and look expectantly to God for healing. Help them change their time schedules to allow God time to work. Help them see that there is life in their marriage by using the office as a metaphor for intimacy and distance. Help them break up destructive distancer-pursuer patterns and enjoy their lives together. Help them restore a vibrant sexual relationship through providing helpful information and limited counseling. Problems in closeness can be healed and a sense of love restored.

Communication

Finishing two hours of tree-cleaning, Jane plops onto a branch and blows a wisp of hair from her eyes.

> Jane: Honey, let's eat at Colonel Colonial's Jungle Fried
>   Chicken tonight.
> Tarzan: Now, dear, you know I don't like to eat chicken
>   meat. It's so, well, so *chicken.* How about Mack's
>   Monkey Burgers?
> Jane: Listen, Wild Man, you better lay off the red meat.
>   You know what the witch doctor said about your
>   cholesterol prob—
> Tarzan: Don't use that tone of voice with me. You
>   sound like my mother.
> Jane: And don't pound your chest in my direction
>   either, you big vegetable. If you did something pro-
>   ductive instead of swinging from the trees all day
>   and having meaningful conversations with
>   Cheetah—
> Tarzan: I'll pound my chest in my tree if I want to. I've
>   had therapy. I know my rights.
> Jane: Will not.
> Tarzan: Will so.
> Jane: Not.
> Tarzan: So.
> Jane: Not.

Once again a famous couple has a communication problem. They end in a bitter disagreement (Tarzan: "So."), both trying to get in the last word (Jane: "Not."). Though it doesn't take much insight to see that Tarzan and Jane have a communication problem, what exactly is wrong with their communication and how could a pastor possibly help them?

Types of Communication Problems

As in any communication problem, there are many ways to understand what is wrong with Tarzan and Jane's communication. It doesn't matter where we begin examining their communication. Their problems started long ago. Tracing the first troublesome communication in the series to Jane (where our excerpt began) will not help Tarzan and Jane solve their problems, as many couples seem to think it will. Those couples spend emotional energy and time trying to pin the blame for starting the disagreement on the spouse. Such efforts are doomed and prevent effective communication or problem-solving.

We will begin to analyze the excerpt from Tarzan and Jane with Jane's first statement.

Misunderstanding Meanings. Jane is tired from cleaning. Perhaps she resents Tarzan's behavior. Instead of expressing her reasons for wanting to eat at Colonel Colonial's, she merely states the request, which invites a factual counter-proposal.

Tarzan is absorbed in his own life—as is Jane. Instead of inquiring about Jane's motivation for wanting to eat out, Tarzan "assertively" expresses his own needs. While Jane might have avoided the disagreement through expressing her reasons for wanting to eat out, Tarzan also could have avoided the disagreement by telling Jane he understood her before he suggested an alternative. He might have said, "Honey, you've worked hard today. In fact, we both have. We deserve to eat out. But remember, I don't like chicken. Can we go somewhere else?"

Jane came back with a "helpful" comment, trying to persuade Tarzan that her solution was for Tarzan's own good. Yet her tone was condescending, suggesting that Tarzan, who had just said he didn't want to appear "chicken," wasn't able to care for himself.

Neither Tarzan nor Jane ever acknowledged the emotional state of the partner. They focused on the content of the decision, becoming quickly embroiled in an argument without conveying to each other that the other person mattered more than the place of dining.

As we discussed in Chapter 4, all communication problems can be seen as being due to misunderstanding the other person's meanings, which conveys a lack of love (failure to value).

Helping the Couple Understand Each Other. A pastor who views Tarzan and Jane's communication difficulties as a misunderstanding of meanings that conveys a lack of valuing might ask Tarzan and Jane to reenact the conversation. "Let me ask you two to begin your discussion one more time," the pastor might say. "Start from when Jane asked you to eat out."

Jane shifts in her chair, then begins. "Tarzan, T-Bird, honey, let's please eat at Colonel Colonial's Jungle Fried Chicken tonight, dear."

Tarzan starts to answer, but the pastor interrupts. "Excuse me, Jane, let me interrupt right there a minute." The pastor notices that Jane presents her communication in a way that she believes to be more palatable, using more endearments and asking please. Yet Jane still fails to help Tarzan understand her motivation for the request. Rather than point out Jane's error, the pastor needs to demonstrate that Tarzan still won't understand Jane's meaning. So the pastor says, "Tarzan, what were you thinking when Jane made that request?"

Tarzan grunts. "It made me mad. I thought she was buttering me up to get her way, trying to be nice so I wouldn't say no. She was manipulating me."

Turning to Jane, the pastor says, "Jane, you didn't want to have that effect on Tarzan, I assume."

"I sure didn't. I was being nice."

"Why don't you tell Tarzan *why* you want to eat out so he'll be able to understand your request better."

"T-Bird, I've been working hard today, sweeping the tree, dusting termites, rearranging branches. I'm pooped. I just want to kick back and veg out tonight instead of slaving over a hot fire cooking supper. Could we eat out at the Colonel's tonight?"

The pastor looks at Tarzan for his response. "Well, Jane, I don't want to eat chicken tonight."

The pastor once again steps in. "Excuse me, Big Guy, but let me ask Jane something. Jane, what did you think about Tarzan's answer to your request?"

Jane blows the hair from her eyes. "He didn't hear me. He didn't even listen."

"Did you hear her?"

"Sure I heard her." Tarzan looks at the pastor and gives an unconscious chest thump.

The pastor notices the sign of agitation but does not respond to it. "Yes, I believe you heard her, but by not letting her know you heard her, you told her that she wasn't important enough to acknowledge." (Two chest thumps. Pastor gulps.) "How might you let her know that you heard?" asks the pastor.

"Jane, I know you're tired, and I appreciate the work you do around the tree house. I care about you and I'd like to take you out, but I don't like chicken. To me, it's a metaphorical communication making me doubt my own maleness and damaging my fragile ego."

"Oh, thank you for being so understanding, dear. I think you're tops. You're swell. I really want to go out and be with you most of all, and I don't have my heart set on chicken. The Colonel's just happened to be the place I thought of first. Let's go someplace else. Pretty please with sugar on it?"

The pastor smiles, gratified at the outcome in which both partners expressed their valuing of the spouse. The pastor realizes what a fantasy Tarzan and Jane's instant insight is. But the pastor is confident that in real life, some progress has been made toward mutual understanding.

Unhelpfully "Punctuating" the Conversation. Tarzan and Jane's communication difficulties could also have been viewed as a problem in "punctuation." Difficulties in communication are like punctuation errors! that distract? and confuse the reader; In the same way that the punctuation errors in the previous sentence confuse the reader, conversational punctuation errors lead to misunderstandings.

For example, if Tarzan continually interrupts, he shows Jane that his own agenda is more urgent than hers, which makes her feel less valued. It is as if he continually intersperses dashes throughout their conversation. A partner who is too dogmatic makes every sentence end with a period, even when there are questions or surprises. On the other hand, some people continually question their spouse, expressing doubt about the spouse's abilities, talents, or behavior. Others use too much silence, failing to express themselves adequately, while their opposites might communicate as if their entire life were a run-on sentence, making the important emotional events in their life nondiscernible. Still others have one crisis after another, punctuating their experiences with so many exclamation points that it is difficult to take their emotional expressions seriously. In each case, the style of communication—regardless of what was said—makes the partner feel devalued.

Helping Couples "Punctuate" Conversations Differently. If you focus on *how* people communicate rather than on *what* they communicate, you might again ask the couple to replay the original disagreement. But instead of asking them to "understand" each other, you would ask them to attend to how they communicate and to whether their communication styles convey love.

For example, in the original conversation between Tarzan and Jane, the pastor might intervene as follows.

Jane: Listen, Wild Man, you better lay off the red meat.
    You know what the witch doctor said about your
    cholesterol prob—
Tarzan: Don't use that tone of voice with me! You
    sound like my mother.
Jane: And don't pound your chest in my direction
    either, you big vegetable.

"Excuse me. May I stop you right here?" The pastor interested in how couples communicate will usually interrupt after short verbal exchanges.

"Tarzan," the pastor might continue, "I noticed that you cut Jane off in the middle of a sentence."

"Well, I've heard the health lecture a thousand times. She gets the Mother-Scolding-Her-Children voice and it's hard for me to take after all these years."

The pastor turns to Jane. "How did you feel when Tarzan interrupted you?"

Jane shifts in her seat. "Well, I didn't like it, and he does it all the time. I know I get on this health kick. I guess I deserve to be interrupted. It doesn't do any good to remind me."

The pastor notices that Jane is not happy with her own behavior, but he focuses on the implications for her self-esteem that arise when Tarzan interrupts her. "I can hear your disappointment in yourself about your own communication, but it seems to me that you really care for your husband."

"I *do* care for him. I want him to be healthy."

"But when Tarzan interrupts you, you feel that those desires are worthless."

"They don't seem to be well received."

Turning to Tarzan, the pastor says, "Tarzan, it appears that when you interrupt, you have an enormous power to make Jane feel worthless."

"Yeah."

"Yet, you both said that Jane continues to be concerned about your health despite your interruption."

"Yeah."

"It seems, then, that your interruption doesn't accomplish what you would like it to. It communicates only that you think what Jane is saying is valueless, but it doesn't get her to stop saying it. Is that what you're trying to accomplish?"

Tarzan squirms. "Of course not. I don't want Jane to feel worthless or to think that she can't talk to me. I'm even glad she cares about my health."

"So even if you think you know what she is about to say, it doesn't help to interrupt her. It causes her to feel negative, devalued, and unloved. She feels that your point is so much more important than hers that she shouldn't even be allowed to express herself."

"Well, I'm not trying to say that. I don't want to listen to a lecture, and I want to convince her that I'm right about where we should eat."

"But even though you're not *trying* to say that her communication is valueless, you *are* communicating it. In fact, you didn't convince her about where to eat."

"That's obvious."

"So by interrupting her, you didn't communicate what you wanted. In fact, you probably made Jane want to prove her worth even more to you. But you did communicate that you devalued her."

"Right. I guess it's not helpful to interrupt."

The pastor says, "I think you've had a good insight, Tarzan. I see that you *want* to improve your marriage. I know it's probably going to be hard for you to change, but your willingness to change is wonderful. I know Jane will be trying equally hard to be tolerant when you slip and interrupt. It won't be easy for her either. Both of you are trying hard to make a better marriage."

The pastor has spent substantial effort helping Tarzan see one way to improve his communication. It is necessary to focus on the deficiencies of his communication, and the pastor knows that Tarzan is likely to feel devalued by the pastor's attempts to help. It is important for the pastor to present criticisms within a positive framework.

Further, having dealt critically with Tarzan over the past few minutes, the pastor should seek to balance the books, looking for an effort to help Jane (perhaps dealing next with her calling Tarzan a "big vegetable"). Without balancing the critical attention between partners over time, the pastor risks having Tarzan feel as if the pastor is "on Jane's side."

Unintended Effects of Communication by the Couple. Another way to view the disagreement between Tarzan and Jane is as an attempt to determine who has power in their marriage. The power that energizes communication difficulties is not economic or physical power. Rather, it is *who can say* what the marriage is going to be like. On each decision, the couple defines and redefines the balance of decisional power in the marriage. On some issues the husband may have more power; on others, the wife; on still others, the power is shared equally. The topic of disagreement is irrelevant.

Tarzan and Jane are locked in a power struggle over who has the power to say how their relationship will be conducted. This is seen by the way the conversation develops into an argument about where they will eat and quickly becomes an argument over whether Tarzan can pound his chest. The topic of the discussion is irrelevant. The important issue for Tarzan and Jane is defining who has the power to say.

Such power struggles lead to poor communication. Tarzan and Jane get sidetracked easily from the topic they are discussing. They try to disempower the partner through put-downs and name-calling. They attempt to convince the other without acknowledging the other's point of view or the emotional significance of the topic to the partner. They cross-complain. They fail to level with the partner or to edit hurtful comments.

Helping Change the Effects of Communication. Paradoxically, it does little good to point out to most couples that they are in a power struggle. Most deny it. They claim only to be "discussing the issues." Rather, allow spouses to see the effects of their communication on the partner. To help partners see their impact, ask each partner what effect he or she desired. Then ask what effect the communication actually had. Show that poor communication devalues the partner, making the partner feel less powerful as a person and consequently making the person strive harder to get his or her "own way." That attitude is diametrically opposed to valuing love.

Devaluing makes partners more contentious. Love and valuing make partners softer, warmer, and more willing to compromise.

The Root of Communication Difficulties

At the root of all communication problems—whether they are understood as misunderstandings, poor communication styles, or attempts to gain power within the marriage—are pride and power.

Pridefully, some communication says, "My agenda is more important than yours. Yours is unimportant to me." Such communication does not *show* the love to the partner that the spouse may actually feel. The partner feels devalued and unimportant.

In other instances, partners want more control of the marriage than they feel they currently have. Feeling insecure or threatened, spouses want to prove that they are adequate, important, and powerful. To do this, they try to control the marriage.

Communication difficulties will not be resolved unless the root causes of pride and power are addressed. Partners must defeat pride and power by valuing the spouse, even if it means laying down one's own expectations and rights. The effort is twofold: to avoid devaluing the spouse and to increase positive evaluations of the partner.

Conflict Management

Most troubled couples have chronic conflict.

Styles of conflict differ radically. Some couples may shout, swear, and physically abuse one another. Some may treat each other with cold disdain. Some may ignore each other, fume acidly, or snipe at each other with painful "zingers." Still others may be experts at character assassination. Regardless of style, couples cannot resolve their differences. Power struggles and hostile devaluing characterize their interactions.

The pastor enters areas of conflict like a soldier in a mine field, fearing a sudden explosion or being afraid that even if a mine is located, it will explode while it is being defused. Yet despite the dangers, mines must be located and defused if the couple is to walk safely.

Agendas

The agenda of the couple is not that of the pastor. A couple in chronic conflict focuses on the issue about which they disagree. They want to resolve the conflict—preferably by winning—and may be disappointed if that doesn't happen. The pastor does not just want to referee disagreements. The pastor wants to help a couple learn how to resolve conflicts by using the principle of faith working through love in which partners value each other despite their differences.

Couples want the pastor to walk with them through the mine field and defuse each mine as it is uncovered. The pastor wants to help the couple disarm a few mines and thus show the couple how to defuse *any* mine they discover.

One implication of the different focus between the counselees and pastor is that you should make your agenda clear up front. Further, repeat the agenda (to help the couple employ faith working through love to resolve *any* differences) often. Couples are easily caught up in specific conflicts, and they forget what the pastor is trying to help them accomplish.

Instituting Your Agenda

Effective conflict resolution will have four sequential steps. Don't skip a step because the partners do not seem able to grasp it or to apply it to their situation.

Step 1: Define the Problem. Initially, help the couple define the problem quickly and not get sidetracked from working on a single problem. One stumbling block to solving problems is failing to agree on what the problem is. When that occurs, the partners spend considerable effort and encounter a great deal of frustration trying to arrive at a single solution to two different problems.

Have each partner state what he or she thinks the main problem is in no more than two sentences. Help the couple determine whether the two statements of the problem are similar or are, in reality, statements about two different problems. If the problem statements are different, get the couple to address each problem separately. Two problems cannot be solved simultaneously.

Have partners state the problem clearly and concretely rather than vaguely and generally. Rather than allowing a husband to define the problem ("You've been a real pain since you got under stress at work"), help him be specific. For example, he could say, "During the last two weeks, you have raised your voice, argued loudly, or criticized me at least four times. I would like for you to act that way less often." Such a concrete statement of the problem tells exactly what he is complaining about and gives a clear statement of what he expects his wife to do to remedy the problem. Obviously, only the husband may think that the wife's behavior is problematic; she may not. Help both partners see that behaviors that bother their spouse will ultimately result in trouble for them if the bothersome behaviors are not dealt with.

Step 2: Help Couples Identify Each Partner's Position. Usually, each person will have a position about how the problem might be solved. Each partner should identify his or her own suggested solution and then summarize the spouse's solution. In our example, the husband says that the wife needs to stop being so crabby. The wife says that the husband needs to be more considerate. If partners summarize their spouse's position, both spouses are sure that their partner values them enough to have heard them. Partners may, in turn, give reasons why they believe their solution is the one that the couple should adopt, but they may not rebut.

If partners do not quickly agree on a proposed solution, which they rarely will, tell them that prolonged discussion of their positions will not help. This is especially true if the issue is one in which incompatible positions have been discussed often.

Step 3: Help Couples Identify the Interests behind their Positions. Generally, people do not want to achieve the particular position that they have offered, even though they might believe that they do. Rather, they want to satisfy their needs and meet the interests behind their position (Fisher and Ury 1981). For instance, in the example above, the husband complained about his wife's crabbiness and took the position that the problem would be solved if she would be less crabby and criticize him less. Behind that position are the interests that he feels demeaned and devalued by his wife's criticism and angry and hurt by her complaints, which extract energy from him and make his life miserable. His wife's position is that he should be more considerate of her. Her interests behind that position are that she feels devalued by her husband's complaints and criticisms; she does not feel understood by her husband; and she wants her husband to agree to help her with more of her chores during stressful times at work.

Step 4: Help Couples Think of a Different Solution That Will Meet Both People's Interests. Let partners brainstorm for solutions that meet the needs of both. Partners suggest solutions that come to mind without evaluating the solutions until brainstorming is complete. Each solution is then evaluated against how well it meets both partners' interests.

Usually, more effective solutions will be thought up if you suggest that each partner try to think of solutions that will meet the partner's interests. People usually find it easy to suggest solutions that meet their own interests and will arrive at those solutions with little difficulty. If the partners are prompted to think of the spouse, less selfish solutions will usually be suggested and final decisions among suggested solutions will be easier.

Goals of Conflict Management Training

The goals of training in conflict management are threefold. Most important is to help partners practice faith working through love, in which they strive to prevent any statement or implication of devaluing and try to positively value the spouse.

Next in importance, partners need to learn a process of resolving conflict that will make it easier to practice faith working through love in future conflict resolution situations. In so doing, partners must develop a mind-set in which they want to solve their problems more than they want to "win" the argument.

Least importantly, partners resolve the issues they discuss in counseling to show that the conflict resolution skills that they have practiced in counseling can work with other problems.

Cognition

Without changed cognition by both partners, changes made in counseling will probably not last.

Help couples change their mental activity in four areas: negative thinking about the marriage, attributions that blame the spouse, expectations about the future of the marriage, and assumptions about the marriage (Baucom and Epstein 1990).

Changing Each Partner's Negative Thoughts

When people seek marital counseling, usually they are discouraged about the relationship. Negative, pessimistic thoughts are fresh on their minds, so it is easy to get people to attend to those thoughts.

Begin by suggesting that how people think controls how they feel and act. Give an example to demonstrate the causal connection between thoughts and actions. For example, suppose a mother sees two of her children, Mary and Ramona, arguing. She corrects them sharply, "You two, stop arguing." Mary thinks, *This is terrible. I'm embarrassed and ashamed.* She apologizes. But Ramona thinks, *It makes me mad when she yells at me. She doesn't understand me. She always takes Mary's side.* Instead of being penitent, Ramona is angry, obstinate, and combative. Both girls heard the same correction, but different thoughts produced different emotions and behaviors.

Tell marriage partners that their negative thinking is partly responsible for their negative feelings about the marriage and their negative behavior toward their spouse. Have them monitor their thoughts during the week, listening as if they had a third ear that could tune into the negative thinking. Encourage them to recognize the negative thinking early and interrupt its flow, replacing negative thinking about the partner and the marriage with positive thinking that emphasizes the partner's good qualities and the benefits of working to preserve the marriage.

Over five counseling sessions, teach counselees to control negative thoughts by thinking about the positive, thinking about how to solve the problem, and noticing ways the partner values the person.

Changing Attributions of Blame

It is natural to explain the causes of our behavior in terms of what we see. If I bump my head on the kitchen cabinet and slam the door in anger, I will probably say that the pain *caused* me to be angry. When marriage partners are in conflict, each sees the other's behavior. They are likely to explain their own behavior as being due to the "terrible" things that the spouse has done to them, blaming the spouse for the marriage difficulties.

The antidote to the poison of blaming is empathy. If partners can see things through the spouse's eyes, then the partners will be less likely to blame the spouse for the problems and will be more likely to take personal responsibility for improving the marriage rather than demanding that the spouse change. Creating such empathy is one of the goals of counseling.

Enhance empathy by emphasizing that each problem has multiple sides. Each person sees the problem from only one side—his or her own perspective. Build the awareness of both partners' different perceptions.

Build that idea from the beginning. Don't just ask each person to describe the problem, ask each to describe the problem from his or her point of view. Throughout counseling, encourage each partner to see things from the spouse's perspective. Have partners describe what they believe their spouse is thinking and feeling. Encourage partners to speculate about how they disturb their spouses. Remind each partner to consider constantly his or her own responsibility in solving the problems rather than talk about his or her partner's failings. Finally, vigilantly help partners see how they can value each other. Partners must think about what the spouse would like and how to give that to the spouse. That requires empathy.

Changing Expectations about the Future of the Marriage

Troubled marriages are plagued by expectations of a dismal future. Often partners can only visualize the marriage continuing in the same painful state as at the present or getting worse. They can't visualize it as ever improving. They feel negatively and selectively perceive only the negative.

One way to break this negative perceptual cycle is to have partners recall a time when their marriage was going positively. This is easy to do when you are taking a relationship history. Have them describe the time in detail, dwelling on the feelings. Ask the partners what they did differently during those times of marital happiness than they currently do. Pose questions: What do you think would happen if you behaved that way again? Could you change things to be more like they were before? What would you have to do differently to get the marriage happy again? Attention to differences between happy and unhappy times and to solutions rather than problems spurs partners to action.

Observe, too, that God is in the full-time business of changing people. He can change each partner to help the couple better their marriage. To the extent that partners are committed to following God, seeking his will, and trying to live their faith through loving the partner, even in difficult situations, God will be more likely to change the marriage into a blessing to both spouses.

Changing Assumptions about the Marriage

For most people, underlying assumptions about marriage are difficult to identify. They are, nonetheless, powerful influencers of behavior. For example, some common assumptions are the following:

1. To demonstrate love, my husband must tell me he loves me several times daily.
2. If I don't feel romantic with my wife, it means we aren't in love any longer.
3. My husband should meet all my needs, especially all my needs for intimacy.

4. My wife should support all my ideas.
5. When I've had a bad day, my husband should be able to sense it and should do something to cheer me up without my having to tell him.
6. My wife should not expect me to be courteous and polite to her. That's what marriage is all about—being yourself and not having to put on some show.
7. My husband should be able to know how to stimulate me when we're making love. I shouldn't have to tell him what to do and when to do it.
8. My wife and I should do almost everything as a couple if we are to maintain a happy marriage.
9. I should be able to keep my partner from ever getting unhappy.
10. My wife and I should never argue or disagree if our marriage is good.

Maladaptive assumptions about the marriage can be changed by following five steps.

First, make the couple aware that much of their behavior is governed by their assumptions about the marriage. Give a copy of the ten listed above and tell the partners why these assumptions may lead to marital problems. Your mere description of the assumptions will not change the partners.

Second, help individuals identify the assumptions in their own marriage. They usually identify most easily the partner's maladaptive assumptions. People are amazingly blind to their own assumptions. Ask about individuals' thoughts about the marriage, which may reveal assumptions. For example, a wife who often thinks, *We're not in love anymore,* might be asked, "How do you know that you aren't in love?" Her reply, "I don't feel any of the excitement I felt when we were in love," might reveal (upon continued discussion) that she believes that love is a feeling. She is confusing romance or passion with love. Love involves more than mere feeling. Feelings may be rebuilt if some of the other elements of love—respect, caring, commitment, knowledge, responsibility, and the will to value—are still present.

Third, once assumptions are identified, examine their consequences. Question the couple to see how holding those assumptions of marriage affects their behavior toward each other. For example, the couple who believe that good marriage is characterized by such a close communion of mind and spirit that communication is not needed may fail to communicate about their sexual experiences, which might lead to the woman failing to have orgasms because she can't tell her husband when to change angles, pressures, or locations of stimulation. If the couple recognize negative consequences of their assumptions, they will be more motivated to change.

Fourth, help individuals change the assumptions that they want to change. When husband or wife recognizes that he or she is making an unwanted assumption, he or she should question the assumption. Avoid having spouses point out their partner's assumptions, regardless how obvious. It is important that each partner takes responsibility for his or her own thoughts, not the spouse's.

Fifth, try to provoke experiences that will make it easier to change assumptions. For example, Mary believed that a "good" marriage was one in which arguing never occurred and that any arguing was evidence of a poor marriage. Mary was eventually assigned "homework." She interviewed at least ten couples whom she considered to be well-adjusted. Her task was to ascertain whether they ever argued. All did. Her interviews made her more willing and able to change her assumptions.

Mary's pastor also questioned the logic of Mary's assumption. Here is a facsimile of their conversation.

Pastor: So, Mary, in a good marriage there is never any
    arguing.
Mary: Right.
Pastor: You and Roger are having difficulty now, but
    have you always had such difficulties?
Mary: No, we had a lot of good years.
Pastor: And you never had a single disagreement
    during all those good years?
Mary: Of course, we had some disagreements.

Pastor: But you were still happy, despite your disagreements. Hmmm. Tell me, can you imagine any couple that could be so angry with each other that they never talked?

Mary: Yes. It wouldn't be a very good marriage.

Pastor: True. But if the couple never talked, they also would never disagree.

Mary: Right. I see what you're getting at. Disagreements don't always mean unhappiness and unhappiness doesn't always mean disagreements.

Pastor: Right. So, what does that tell you about your assumption?

Mary: It probably isn't correct. But still it isn't good to fight continually.

Pastor: That's true, and naturally, you want to avoid fighting, arguing, or even getting angry at each other. Still, saying that you want to resolve disagreements is far different than believing that you can never disagree with your husband and that any disagreement means you have a poor marriage.

Mary: You're right. There is a big difference.

Summary

Changing people's thoughts will help changes be more lasting. Help partners recognize negative thoughts and replace them with thoughts about how each is valuing the other. Help partners avoid blaming each other by getting them to think of their own behavior and how they can improve it. Help them focus on faith working through love, giving a brighter expectation of the future of their marriage. Finally, help them identify and change assumptions about the marriage that drag them down. As they change their way of viewing the marriage, they will be able to avoid harmful devaluing and promote positive valuing.

8

Engagement Stage:
Covenant and Commitment

Two understandings of commitment permeate modern culture—
one based on contract, one on covenant. Covenantal commitment
is more traditional and scriptural, but contractual commitment is
steadily prevailing (Bromley and Busching 1988).

People who treat commitment as contractual may be highly
committed to their careers, marriages, friends, or their Christianity. Yet contractual commitment is more fragile than is covenantal commitment.

Contracts and Covenants

Contractual commitment depends on reciprocity or exchange.
Strong ties are forged in relationships when partners exchange
things valued positively or when partners share resources needed
by the spouse. Commitment is built on mutual need fulfillment.
When needs are not fulfilled, commitment can erode.

The traditionally Christian concept of marital commitment is
built on a different foundation. A Christian's commitment to God

precedes Christian marital commitment. God made a unilateral covenant with those who believe in him, to love and care for them forever. The covenant was first articulated with Abraham and later ratified through Jesus Christ's death and resurrection. Christians respond to God's unilateral, covenantal love with faithful love. Christians make their own human covenant with God by partaking of the communion meal (see John 6:53–54). Paul likens marriage to the covenantal relationship between Christ and the church (Eph. 5:25–33; see also 1 Cor. 6:16–17). In a covenant, both parties promise to love self-sacrificially, placing the other person's welfare at least equal to and sometimes above one's own welfare.

Contract commitment, based on exchange of resources, is individualistic. Each person meets his or her obligations only as long as there is a reasonable likelihood that eventually the other person will meet his or her obligations. Each person is mainly concerned with receiving the resources that the contract stipulates, which are his or her rights.

Covenantal commitment leads to a concern for the welfare of the other person. People care for and stay committed to a partner because they have staked their honor, their word, and their identity on fulfilling their covenantal obligations toward the other person regardless of what the other person does or doesn't do.

Some people live as if they have a contractual relationship with God. They love and honor him as long as they believe that he will meet their needs. If they think God isn't going to meet their needs, they may sue God for breach of contract in the court of public opinion by proclaiming that God let them down.

In a covenant, a person honors God because he or she believes God and has pledged to honor him. Whether the person thinks God will meet his or her needs is irrelevant to covenantal behavior. Covenantal love of God is a matter of one's honor, word, and identity and not of what benefits God offers.

A person who lives as if he or she has a contractual relationship with God may see marriage as a contract also. One who has a covenantal relationship with God will more likely see marriage as a covenant with the spouse.

Increasing Commitment

Generally, in marriage counseling, there is a need for the pastor to promote increased commitment. Whether commitment is based on contract or covenant, is strong or weak, marital stresses and strains erode commitment.

Help Partners Meet Each Other's Needs

People usually feel more committed if they believe their needs are adequately met and they are valued as loved ones. The pastor can help the couple strengthen commitment to each other by helping them see how they meet each other's needs and how they value each other.

Anything that promotes more satisfaction with the marriage will strengthen commitment to it. As you help the couple build faith working through love, the partners will strengthen their commitment.

Eliminate Competitors to the Marriage

Eliminating competitors to a relationship will strengthen commitment to the relationship. Competitors may be other romantic interests or activities that interfere with the couple's relationship. This might include work, hobbies, or even church activities.

Share Resources

Sharing resources strengthens commitment because neither person wants to give up the resources held in common. In marriage, resources held in common include anything in which a couple invests time, energy, and money—a jointly owned house or other property, children, mutual hobbies, and leisure activities. Even a couple's identity as a couple is a resource. The more couples are thought of by others as couples, the more their identity as such is strengthened.

Use Contracts If You Must

Contracts are not necessarily to be shunned. If one partner is Christian and one is not or both are not Christians, a contract can often bring harmony and stability to troubled relationships. Duties and expectations can be made clear through the negotiation of a contract. In one couple, the wife (a new Christian) agreed not to make the husband (a non-Christian) feel guilty or morally inferior by bringing judgments on him for failing to attend church, drinking, and swearing. The husband promised not to belittle the wife's faith, prevent her from attending church, or judge her as mentally inferior for holding to the faith. In that case, the contract prevented the lack of valuing that had emerged following the wife's recent conversion to Christianity.

Minimize a Heavy-Handed Emphasis on God's Laws

Marriage was designed by God as a permanent relationship that mirrors the permanent faithfulness of God to the believer. Many verses describe God's desire for the permanence of marriage (Mal. 2:16; Matt. 5:32; 19:9; Mark 10:6-9; 1 Cor. 7:15). It is tempting to quote verses to partners whose commitments are wavering and to command that they obey.

At times, that may be the very tack to take. Probably, though, that approach should be taken less often than it is. There are several reasons for this. First, Christian commitment is based on covenant, not law. Commanding obedience to law reinforces a contractual view of marriage, which can undermine commitment in the long run. Second, people inevitably make attributions about why they remain together. When obedience to God's laws is stressed, people say that they are staying together only because they *must* according to God's law. That makes it more difficult for them to see that they are also staying together because they love each other. Third, people do not usually respond well to coercion. Some may rebel, especially if the pastor's style is heavy-handed.

Assume a Lifelong Commitment

Once a couple, Christian or non-Christian, express their verbal commitment to each other, strengthen their resolve to work on the marriage by pointing out instances of their commitment. Assume they will be together forever and therefore need to reconcile any differences. One powerful means of helping solidify commitment is presupposing their lifelong commitment.

Promote Covenantal Commitment to God

For the Christian, the pastor will want to move toward a covenantal rather than a contractual view of marriage. The foundation of the covenantal perspective on marriage is the individual Christian commitment of the spouses. To the extent that individuals can understand the covenant of God and can apply that perspective to their own marriage, the commitment can be strengthened.

Teach about Covenants

One way to help Christians understand covenant is through teaching about it. This is best accomplished in classes, groups, or sermons rather than through counseling. However, there may be times for discussing covenants during counseling if partners are unfamiliar with the concept.

The Joshua Intervention

At the end of counseling, commitment is cemented by the "Joshua intervention." In the same way that Joshua built a memorial to the Lord to celebrate God's bringing the children of Israel across the Jordan River into the promised land, encourage couples who have completed counseling to create a memorial to the Lord for what he has done in their marriage. They may establish an annual ritual to commemorate successful marital counseling, or they may create a symbol to remind them of what God has done in their marriage. One couple went on an annual ski trip each winter to celebrate their successful counseling. Another took a weekend vacation away from the children to renew their love. Another couple bought a beautiful box in which they each placed a small scroll stating their desire to honor God by making their marriage a reflection of his ever-faithful covenantal love for Christians and for the church.

The Case of Bonnie

Bonnie felt drained after her second session with Pastor Buck. Delving into her family history had been illuminating, but her emotions were still in turmoil five hours after the meeting. She had seen patterns in her family that she had never acknowledged before. Her father's rejection of her when she failed to make all A's and B's, his obvious displeasure when she decided to work instead of go to college, and his open disgust when she told him that she had eloped and married Walter at age 19 were vivid in her mind. The way Pastor Buck had made her visualize the scenes helped because it brought to mind the power of her father's facial expressions to manipulate her.

Her father's rejections still hurt. Buck's suggestion that Jesus could help her forgive her father didn't take away the pain. Even though she still hurt, Bonnie felt a release from some of the buried bitterness she had harbored toward her father in the four years following his death. *Forgiveness*, she mused, *must take time*. She drew another deep breath and felt it catch in her chest.

She also had new insight into herself. Wanting to please her father with the success that he valued so highly, she had nagged, berated, and bullied Walter into higher-status jobs than he had wanted to take. Yet the more she had pushed, the more Walter had dug in his heels. The more he failed to meet Bonnie's expectations, the more disgusted she became with him and his apparent lack of ambition. Finally, she had given up. Then Walter seemed to catch fire. His ambition sprouted like weeds in a garden, driving him away from her and into work and achievement. It was funny how her parents' behaviors were now replaying themselves in her life. Her father had been ambitious and driven, while her mother had nagged him persistently to give more to the family and less to his work. While the early years of Bonnie and Walter's marriage had seemed exactly the opposite, Bonnie now saw the duplication.

Bonnie puttered around the house, picking up toys from the living room, chatting with Cheryl, dusting—marking time until Walter came home from work.

Darkness fell, and with it large flakes of snow began to float down. Cheryl was put to bed. Bonnie sat in front of the window, rocking, covered by a blanket, holding a mug of hot chocolate and an open book, which she could not seem to read.

As the snow accumulated, so did her anxiety. Where was Walter? Her concern mixed with plans of imminent confrontation. She was going to ask Walter to attend counseling with her.

The Jeep Cherokee dieseled to an asthmatic-sounding stop in the driveway. Silence. Walter stamped through the door, complaining of the cold, the snow, the traffic, and the drivers. It didn't seem to Bonnie that it was an ideal time for a confrontation.

Dinner passed. Walter talked. Bonnie chewed, nodded, and said one or two words at the right times, her mind occupied with the upcoming fight over counseling.

"Honey," she said as she cleared the plates, "I went to counseling with Pastor Buck this morning."

"Um hmmm. How was it?"

"It was real good. I got a lot out of it. I learned a lot about my family, especially Dad's rejection of me. I think it has a lot to do with the strains we've felt."

"Wait a minute," said Walter. "You mean, strains *you've* felt. I don't think there's anything wrong with our marriage that couldn't be fixed by having you simply stop complaining and worrying so much about my work. You always wanted me to be a big-shot, and now that a little success seems within my grasp, you start complaining. *That's* the problem."

Bonnie picked up the ice cream dipper and dug into a hard frozen brick of fudge ripple. "Pastor Buck helped me to see that a lot of that is true. I think he might be able to help you, too, if you'd come to counseling with me. I think we need—"

"No. I told you before, if you want to waste your time going to counseling with the old guy, that's fine with me, but don't try to make me waste my time. I'm too busy, and I don't need another sermon each week."

"It's not a waste of time, and he doesn't give ser—"

"I don't want to talk about this. We've had this conversation before. I'm not going to counseling. You need to get your act together and get the pressure off me. That's what our marriage really needs."

Bonnie slammed the bowl of ice cream in front of Walter. "Has it ever occurred to you that our troubles are not all my fault?"

"Don't start throwing food around and getting all irrational. I told you that our 'problems,' as you call them, are way overblown in your mind. We're doing okay. Lots of people are doing worse. Look at the *Groehlings*. Carl's an elder and he and Katherine hardly speak to each other civilly in public. Heaven only knows what they're like when they're alone."

"You're deflecting us away from the issue. It doesn't matter how the Groehlings are doing. *We* need to get some help for *our* marriage. We—"

"I already told you. I'm not going to any counseling. I'm not even sure it's good for you to be spending so much time around church and that old pastor. I think it's poisoning your mind. I don't feel like eating any dessert now either." Walter picked up the bowl of ice cream, carried it across the kitchen, and dumped it into the cat's bowl.

"Don't walk away from me like that," said Bonnie.

"I'm going back to work," said Walter. He grabbed his coat from the rack, snatched his briefcase from the couch, and jerked open the door. A burst of icy air rushed across the room and slapped Bonnie.

"Wait." called Bonnie. The door slammed.

No further arguments occurred that week, though Bonnie and Walter felt continual tension. Both pretended the argument had not happened.

After Bonnie's third session with Buck, neither felt encouraged about Bonnie's marriage. The session had not gone particularly well. Buck had addressed Bonnie's difficulty with closeness. Much of her conflict and communication with Walter centered on their use of time. They generally avoided conflict and avoided being with each other. Bonnie and Walter each feared intimacy. At the beginning of the interview, she blamed Walter completely, saying that she wanted more intimacy, but Walter selfishly wouldn't provide it. Later, though, she began to see that she had a selfish attitude about her own time and energy. It was in part, her selfishness about having more independence that spurred her to drive Walter to high productivity.

Discouraged about herself, she left the counseling session. She had seen the selfish motives that prevented her from honoring and valuing Walter.

She spent a day alone, struggling with God. She became convinced that she needed to talk with Walter about their problems.

She could not work up the courage to face him again until he stayed at work until ten o'clock one night. When he came home, she was waiting for him.

Walter tossed his hat on the rack and shucked out of his coat. "Are you still up? I didn't expect you'd be up so late."

Bonnie gave Walter a hug. Over his shoulder, she said, "I haven't had any time to talk with you all week, and I was feeling deprived." They parted.

Later, as Walter finished a late snack, he said, "You seem happier lately."

Bonnie poured him another glass of milk. "Some. I still worry about our marriage."

"You're not going to start up again, are you?"

"No. I've been practicing the advice that Pastor Buck gave me. He said that I ought to pray more and complain less." She sat down across from Walter. "I was pretty discouraged after my last meeting with him."

"Why?"

"We talked about intimacy. I had always thought of myself as needing a lot of intimacy. I had mostly blamed you for somehow not meeting my needs."

"Don't start that again. I'm different from you. I don't need as much intimacy."

"That's one of the things I talked about with Pastor Buck. He convinced me that I didn't need as much intimacy as I thought I needed. I demanded closeness from you, knowing you'd not give it to me. It kept us at arm's length. Anyway, as I thought about my conversation with Pastor Buck and prayed about you and me, I knew Pastor Buck was right."

Walter finished his snack and drained the glass of milk. "Maybe you are learning some good things about yourself from counseling after all," he said.

Two days later, at the fourth counseling session, Bonnie told Buck about her conversation with Walter. "He seemed glad that I was learning things about myself. Honestly, though, he was so smug about the whole thing. He thinks that we have hardly any problems, and even if we have a problem, it is totally my fault. I get so angry I could bite nails."

"What did you do when he said the problem was your fault?" said Buck.

"He didn't say it. He implied it. Anyway, I practiced what you had suggested—not complaining, but praying. It worked. At least I didn't blow up."

Buck shifted in his chair. "I hope I didn't say, 'Don't complain, just pray.' That isn't exactly what I want you to learn. I want you to gain spiritual maturity through these difficulties."

"I think I am. Praying is less mechanical now, and my whole source of happiness isn't tied to my marriage any longer. I realize that my relationship with the Lord is my real source of happiness."

"Great."

Buck and Bonnie spent the remainder of the session brainstorming ways that Bonnie might exercise her faith within her marriage. They talked of ways that she could show love to Walter without making Walter feel that she was demanding more intimacy from him.

Talk soon turned to Walter's seeming obsession with work. Bonnie recognized how she had driven him toward work, but she still worried that Walter's overcommitment to work would eventually split their marriage. She felt she had become less important to Walter than his work. Bonnie decided that the topic needed to be broached with Walter. For 10 minutes, Bonnie practiced talking with Pastor Buck as if he were Walter. Bonnie left the session determined to talk with Walter about his use of time.

At 11:05 P.M., Pastor Buck's phone rang.

"Pastor Buck, this is Bonnie." Her voice shook.

"What's wrong?"

"I talked with Walter tonight. We had a long talk, in fact, about our marriage."

"And that upset you?"

"A lot of things were positive. He said he thought I had a softer attitude and seemed to be growing closer to the Lord. I asked him to come to counseling this Wednesday, and he flatly said no. He said he had an important meeting then. He said to stop trying to get him to counseling, that he didn't need it and he didn't want me to nag him about it again. I feel like the door has been slammed in my face."

Buck consoled Bonnie for 10 minutes. He reminded her of the progress she and Walter had made in their marriage and of the progress she had made in her spiritual life.

When he hung the phone up, Pastor Buck felt drained. While he tried to stay confident and positive with Bonnie, he was also discouraged about Walter's failure to respond to the many positive changes in Bonnie during the last four weeks. He sat down in the chair beneath his reading lamp, closed his eyes, and began to pour out his heart to God on behalf of Bonnie and Walter.

9

Disengagement Stage: Moving Back to Pastoral Care

Martha had been in counseling with Pastor Smithers for seven weeks. Martha felt better able to cope with her three time-consuming children, part-time job, and demands as a wife.

Carefully, Pastor Smithers broached the topic of ending counseling. Martha cried a little at the loss of support, but Pastor Smithers firmly insisted, and they ended counseling. Martha missed church that Sunday. And the next, and the next. By the time Pastor Smithers noticed her absence among the congregation of 300, it had been seven weeks. A phone call to Martha netted a brush-off.

At a Christian businessmen's luncheon two months later, Pastor Smithers cornered Martha's husband, who angrily described how shabbily the pastor had treated Martha—not caring for her and finally rejecting her. Martha had sought fellowship at First Lutheran Church, where people *really* cared about her.

Pastor Smithers was so flabbergasted that he couldn't respond to Martha's husband. He recalled the hours of ministry to Martha over the five years she attended his church, times of special ministry when her mother died, the over 10 hours of counseling about her marital tensions. The more he thought about her actions, the more outraged and hurt he became. It was months before he could function without anger, and the scars remained for years.

The Tasks of Disengagement

Such scenarios are not uncommon in pastoral ministry. They are born of violated expectations between pastor and parishioner. Pastors tend to protect themselves emotionally from such traumas by labeling the parishioner as being "sick" or sinful. It helps keep the pastoral ego intact.

Sometimes the fault for misunderstandings lies with the parishioner, but sometimes the pastor contributes by not making a schedule for disengagement explicit. Many misunderstandings can be avoided.

The tasks of disengagement are threefold:

- Solidify attitudes of confession and forgiveness.
- Help counselees leave counseling and return to their normal activities.
- Plan for spiritual growth.

Accomplishing these tasks will smooth the way for disengagement.

Solidifying Confession and Forgiveness

Counseling helps participants see their own responsibilities in making the marriage what it is—troubled or healed.

Assuming Too Much Responsibility

While you want to promote an attitude of responsibility that allows each partner to work to improve the troubled marriage, you can promote an attitude of assuming too much responsibility.

Maria had an affair with a co-worker. When she and William sought counseling with their pastor to deal with the aftermath of the affair, they described a history of emotional hurt and mutual rejection. Both agreed that the affair was as much William's responsibility as it was Maria's. Maria had even forgiven William for pushing her into the affair. William was having a hard time forgiving Maria, which was the focus of their request for counseling.

Their pastor interpreted their situation differently. He said that both people were responsible for the distressed marriage, but not for the affair. "There are many ways to deal with a distressed marriage," he said. "Maria chose to have an affair to deal with the troubles. She is responsible for that choice and needs to come before God with a contrite heart, confessing her sin and repenting of it."

Because of their pastor's gentle confrontation, Maria could accept full responsibility for the affair. Maria's acceptance of her legitimate responsibility helped to restore trust. Naturally, her mere confession did not instantly restore trust. After an affair, trust is regained slowly. However, Maria's confession began the restoration of trust, which had been stymied when both partners felt responsible for the breach of faithfulness.

Each person is responsible for what he or she does within a marriage. Failings need to be dealt with by confessing them to the Lord and bringing the blood of Jesus to bear on them. Only with confession and repentance will there be healing and forgiveness.

True Responsibility Is to Confess One's Part

Within a troubled marriage, each person is hurt. Therefore, each person is responsible for forgiving the other person, whom he or she perceives as having inflicted the hurt. Forgiveness should occur in private prayer to God unless specifically invited by the spouse. Third parties, such as friends or relatives, should not be involved.

Ideally, forgiveness restores relationships, if the forgiveness is sought and received. Thus, for the relationship to be fully restored, each person should confess his or her part of the marital troubles to the spouse and should seek forgiveness for those acts.

Promoting Confession and Forgiveness

From the beginning of counseling, partners are asked to reflect on their own failings rather than on their spouse's failings. Partners are expected to speak for themselves. When they speak for their spouses, interrupt tactfully and encourage them to tell their own stories.

Build an attitude of personal responsibility that will allow each partner to confess his or her own shortcomings. At the beginning of counseling, the attitude of personal confession usually goes against the grain. As you lovingly and discretely insist on each person taking responsibility for what he or she can change, an attitude of confession grows.

Sometimes the partners are ready to deal with confession and forgiveness as early as the second or third session. If the poisons of unforgiveness and bitterness can be drained early in counseling, then solutions are more readily accepted during later sessions. However, many couples are not ready to confess their failures until later.

By the fourth or fifth session, an attitude of confession may have been built. Confession and forgiveness may be hastened by using a discrete intervention to promote confession and forgiveness (see Worthington and DiBlasio 1990). In the fourth session, partners are asked to reflect during the week on whatever they would like to confess to their partner. In the fifth session, each takes turns confessing a way that he or she has hurt the other. Forgiveness should be granted only if the partner really feels that he or she can forgive the spouse.

At the end of the session, comment on the courage required for partners to confess their faults to each other. Discuss James 5:13–16. For example, you might say:

> It says in James, "Is any of you suffering?"—and you both have been suffering. It says, "Let him pray. Is any cheerful? Let him sing praise. Is any among you sick?" Your marriage certainly qualified as being ill when we began to work together. "Let him call the elders of the church"—which is what you did when you came to me for counseling—"and let them pray over him, anointing him with oil in the name of the Lord; and the prayer of faith will save the sick man"— or the sick marriage in this case—"and the Lord will raise him up; and if he has committed sins, he will be forgiven. Therefore, confess your sins to one another." You have each done this. It continues, "Pray for one another, that you may be healed. The prayer of a righteous man has great power in its effects." I believe that you have begun to heal your marriage by confessing your part in the marital troubles to each other. Now, it would help if you pray for each other.

Promoting forgiveness in this instance involves the use of a technique and ritual, but promoting forgiveness also involves the personality, style, and love of the pastor. Technique alone will not persuade couples to forgive each other. Couples forgive when one partner becomes vulnerable and the other partner treats that vulnerability sensitively. By doing this, the couple communicates valuing to each other. They show faith working through love.

Throughout counseling, look for instances of valuing and call each partner's attention to those instances in a way that invites emotional participation by the partners. Your voice should be soft. Your eye contact should include both partners. Your expression should be open and caring.

By your nonverbal and verbal expressions, you say, "I see that you care for each other. This is evidence of your love and valuing. You are trying hard to love each other and heal your marriage. I have just seen something important happen between you." Your attitude, behavior, and words will then mark the confession and forgiveness as important, helping make it truly significant for each partner.

Forgiveness is the ultimate form of valuing. More than any other action, it places the needs of the other person and the desire to restore broken relationships above the selfish desires of self-vindication and bitterness. Confessing and forgiving others is the core of faith working through love.

Helping Counselees Return to Normal Activities

Facilitate the couple's getting back to normal. Getting back to normal can be less painful if expectations about counseling are addressed from the beginning of counseling and are reiterated at the beginning of each session.

The inexorable approach of the final session of counseling may stimulate some predictable behaviors in some counselees. Counselees who are anxious about being abandoned may perceive the last session as abandonment by the pastor. Even if the pastor is clear from the outset about the five-session limit, issues of intimacy often arise for clients who have had difficulty with intimacy in the past. It might smooth the transition back to normality if you predict that ending formal counseling might be difficult.

Sometimes people will have crises at or before the last session or just after it in an unconscious attempt to prolong counseling. While some professional therapists rigidly insist that additional counseling not be offered in crisis, most therapists will see a client in crisis for an additional session to control the crisis, but they won't extend their regular counseling contacts with the person.

Pastors have an ongoing relationship with the person, whereas professionals will likely never see the counselee again. This makes the threat of abandonment by the pastor less severe than by the psychotherapist. Nonetheless, some counselees strongly resist termination and react emotionally to it. On the other hand, a pastor can't simply abandon a needy parishioner simply because he or she has attended five counseling sessions. Pastors must develop a trustworthy referral list for long-term counseling, which allows them to resume normal pastoral care with the person or couple (but not interminable counseling).

Suggesting referral communicates that you are not abandoning the couple, while it also avoids unhealthy dependence on you. Pastoral counseling should aim to help people depend on God, not the pastor or a professional counselor.

Promoting Spiritual Growth

The main point of pastoral counseling is to help people solve their marital difficulties within a Christian context. It helps them understand problems within the context of their Christian life and apply the principle of faith working through love to solve the problem. If this does not happen, pastoral counseling cannot be considered a success.

Evidences of Spiritual Growth

The easiest visible evidence of spiritual growth is the way that people respond during counseling. Although in-session behavior is easy to see, it is not necessarily a reliable indication that long-term spiritual growth has occurred. Look for evidence of how people react outside of counseling. How do spouses report that their partners behave between sessions? How do interactions with others within the congregation appear? Do they pray and seek the will of God with more maturity than previously? Do they show an increased capacity for self-sacrificial love?

The person's emotional state can also indicate his or her spiritual maturity. If the person can accept his or her situation better, regardless of whether the outcome is going well, then the person is likely learning that God is the source of peace and joy, not getting one's way.

Promoting Spiritual Maturity

The pastor promotes a spiritual, Christian perspective on problems and their solution throughout counseling. The way the difficulties are conceptualized, the way the pastor supports the person, the way the pastor encourages the person to respond to the difficulties help promote spiritual maturity.

Nonetheless, ending counseling is a chance for lessons to be reemphasized. The person or couple can be asked to reflect on what has been learned during counseling. The pastor might encourage the people to apply the lessons by describing other ways they intend to improve the marriage. Each suggestion should be related to how it demonstrates a valuing of the other person that shows faith working through love. Planning concrete actions for the future is probably the best way for the couple to exhibit their spiritual maturity.

Still, planning concrete actions is pastoral *counseling*. The pastor must move the couple into a pastoral *care* situation, which will involve helping the couple be more involved with spiritually mature members of the congregation or at least with others who are struggling to grow spiritually. Small-group ministry of the church is probably the best way for the couple to receive such supportive fellowship. For information about discipleship groups developed by McMurry (1983, 1985), write to Christ Presbyterian Church, 2508 Dickens Road, Richmond, VA 23230.

The Case of Bonnie

Pastor Buck gazed out his window. The snow was finally beginning to melt. The slush was piled, gritty-brown, along all the streets.

Cars had bulldozed their way from underneath, and the street glistened. Bonnie hustled across the street toward the church and walked flat-footed over the mashed-down snow on the sidewalk. A moment later, Bonnie sat in the black recliner across from Buck's old desk chair.

"Sorry for calling you so late the other night. I was just so discouraged. It's easy to be depressed late at night—especially when you feel you've been kicked in the face."

"You seemed pretty dejected because Walter wouldn't come to counseling," he said.

"I was. I'm still disappointed. I thought we were making such great progress on our marriage. At least *I* was feeling better about it. I expected that we'd come to counseling on this final session and we'd work everything out and live happily ever after." She laughed bitterly. "Fairy tale. Wrong on all counts. I know Walter had an important meeting, and I'm more rational about it now, but at nearly midnight, I wasn't thinking plainly."

"And what are you thinking now?"

Bonnie rubbed a slender hand over her forehead. "I had some unrealistic thoughts. At least we haven't argued for days. We seem to be doing better, but we're not at the happily-ever-after stage by a long shot."

"That sounds more realistic."

Talk turned to Bonnie's efforts to make fewer demands on Walter's time. Five minutes later, three raps on the door interrupted their talk. Buck rose slowly and shuffled across the office. He opened the door about eight inches.

"Hey, Walter," he said.

"Uh, Pastor Buck, is Bonnie here?"

"Sure," said Buck. He let the door swing open. Walter craned his head around the corner peering into the room. Bonnie looked over her shoulder at Walter.

"Honey, you asked if I'd come to counseling with you, and, uh, well, would you mind if I—?" he paused.

"I thought you had an important meeting," said Bonnie.

"I did, but I, uh, canceled it."

"Why don't you come on in, Walter, and sit?" said Buck.

Walter dragged a chair near to Bonnie's. "I was kind of a jerk the other night," he said to Bonnie. "I knew it was important that I come with you, but I was thinking with my billfold rather than my heart."

Bonnie reached out and put her hand on Walter's. Walter put his other hand on top of Bonnie's. Bonnie's eyes were tearful. "I'm glad you wanted to come. What about your meeting?"

"I'll try to reschedule. If I can't, well, what the hey." His voice was husky.

Bonnie squeezed Walter's hand.

"What made you change your mind, if you don't mind my asking?" said Buck.

"I've been thinking about how Bonnie has behaved since beginning counseling. I'd have to say I've been impressed with her softness. That made a big difference. I've felt guilty about rejecting her offer to come to counseling. I wrestled with the idea all week and finally decided last night, during a time of prayer. I felt that I should come today, so this morning at work, I called off the appointment."

Buck grinned. "It sure makes me feel warmer'n a flat rock in July that you're here. I know Bonnie feels the same. I can see that you both are becoming more open to the Holy Spirit's leading in your lives."

Pastor Buck turned to Bonnie. "You told me earlier that you'd learned a lot of things about yourself in the last few weeks but you hadn't had the chance to tell Walter."

Bonnie nodded and looked at Walter. "I've not been a bargain to live with. I pushed and nagged you when we were first married, wanting you to be more ambitious. Then when you got involved with your job, I got angry about that and nagged you about working too long. I feel like the world's biggest nag. I'm sorry. I'm going to try, with God's help, to accept you as you are and stop trying to make you into something else. I hope you can forgive me."

Walter looked at Bonnie. Then his eyes teared. "Honey, I've not been a bargain myself. I've not been sensitive to your feelings at all. Whatever you've wanted, I've been against. If you're serious about accepting me, I'll try to give you more of the respect I feel for you."

"You really respect me?" she asked.

"I always have. You're a strong woman. I've always known that. In fact, that's partly why I married you. I like that part of you. It complements me, and I think that's how God wanted marriage to work. Isn't that right, Pastor?"

"You don't need my confirmation on that. Y'all are doing great. You're both expressing a desire to change your attitude toward each other. You're saying that you prize each other, that you value each other. That's the essence of marriage and even of the Christian life. How is this attitude going to show up in how you treat each other?"

Walter said, "I'm going to make sure that Bonnie knows that I love her more than I love my work. Even if I have to work long hours, I want her to know that she's number one with me."

"How is she going to know that?"

"I guess if I have to work long hours, I need to tell her that I still love her. Maybe if I have to work extra, we can plan something special that we can do as a reassurance of our love for each other." He turned to Bonnie. "How does that sound?"

"Sounds great."

Buck looked at Bonnie. "How about you? How is your new attitude going to show up?"

Walter jumped in before Bonnie could speak. "I think it's already been showing up. Her actions have been softer, less judgmental for the last few weeks."

"I want to continue that," said Bonnie. "I want to give you the space you need, and I'll be committed to our marriage, no matter what."

"That's good to hear. I had worried about your commitment," said Walter.

Bonnie looked directly at Walter. "I think my commitment was a little shaky a while back. Even Cheryl sensed it. She cried every time I went into another room. That began to worry me. Pastor Buck helped me see that her crying might be her insecurity about whether I would be around for her. That shook me. It made me want to work on our marriage."

She shifted in her chair until she was almost facing Walter. "I worried about your commitment for a while, too. I thought you might be having an affair with someone at work." She paused, holding her breath.

Walter shook his head and pursed his lips. "There's no woman I would even look at twice."

"Deep down I knew that," said Bonnie. "It was my own struggle with commitment that bothered me. Still, it's good to hear you say there isn't anyone else."

"Only you, honey."

Pastor Buck said, "You both seem committed to the marriage and willing to try to make some changes to improve your marriage. I wonder what you've learned out of this difficult time in your marriage?"

Bonnie was the first to speak. "I've thought about that for a few weeks. I learned that God never leaves us. More than that. God will hound us if we coast away from him. He hounded me right back to him, which helped me see our marriage in a different light."

"I learned that troubles can be a time in which faith is built rather than torn apart. I learned that by watching this wonderful wife of mine deal with her problems with me. It made a big impact on me."

Bonnie said, "I owe a lot of that to counseling with Pastor Buck. I learned that his support and encouragement and his faithful Christian witness throughout our difficulties kept me interested in Christ. His commitment to the Lord buoyed up my commitment to the Lord."

Pastor Buck smiled. "I guess that's what counseling is all about, isn't it?"

Part **3**

Application

10

A Suggested Five-Session Plan

What happens in each session of Strategic Pastoral Marital Counseling? We provide an outline for each session, using three headings: (1) goals and focus; (2) suggested activities; and (3) important points. We view this chapter as one to which you might refer as you prepare for counseling each week. To refresh your memory of the details of specific interventions, refer to previous chapters.

First Session: Engagement

Goals and Focus

The goals of the first session are to engage the individual or couple through establishing a relationship, joining them in working on the marriage, and assessing the major areas of their marriage and their level of Christian maturity. You will also provide hope for change through referring to God's promises in the Scriptures, personal testimony, and prayer. The contacts will be structured so the parties are clear about how often and for how long the meetings will take place. You will introduce the theme of the sessions—to

149

build the partners' faith and capacity for love as it manifests itself in their marriage.

Suggested Activities

To promote a good working relationship, you must accomplish two tasks:

- Structure counseling by clearly describing the five-session format.
- Join the couple or individual partner in trying to improve the marriage by (1) conveying warmth, caring, and helpfulness, and (2) promoting agreement on tasks and goals.

Generally, accomplishing these tasks will require not only friendliness but a relatively task-focused approach to the interview.

Begin by asking each counselee to describe the problem from his or her point of view. Get a brief (five minutes or less) bird's eye view of the current status of the marriage; then, if you believe that counseling would be helpful, describe the five-session approach of Strategic Pastoral Marital Counseling and solicit the counselee's agreement.

Then begin to explore the problem in detail. Assess each of the following areas:

- Each partner's Christian beliefs and values and his or her Christian maturity
- Each partner's core vision of marriage
- How readily each partner confesses his or her own part in the marital troubles, how much each blames the other, and how willing each is to forgive
- How closeness is handled
- Areas of poor communication
- Style of conflict resolution, including topics of frequent disagreement and how emotionally charged each topic is
- Cognition about the marriage, including assumptions, expectations, perceptions, attributions of cause, and negative self-talk

- Degree of commitment to the marriage and to counseling and whether commitment is based on a contractual or covenantal understanding
- Complicating factors such as affairs, alcohol and drug abuse, or physical abuse.

Don't use these factors as a checklist, which you proceed to work down with mechanical precision. Rather, listen to the couple discuss their relationship and use the checklist to guide exploratory questions and to fill in gaps that are not discussed spontaneously.

Assign activities between sessions. It is important to orient the counselees to your approach to counseling as early as possible. Assign couples to read the first five chapters of *Value Your Mate*.

Important Points

Establish a good pastoral counseling relationship, which is probably the key to effective pastoral counseling. Further, begin from the outset to focus on valuing and devaluing in the relationship.

Don't let negative communication prevail. Balance weaknesses with strengths, discouragement with hope.

At the end of the first session, recap what you have learned, placing problem areas into a framework of Christian love and characterizing the task of counseling as to restore love to their marriage by helping them value each other more and devalue each other less. You should have a sense of the area that partners believe to be the major area—usually conflict, communication, or closeness. State your perception and see whether the partners agree.

Direct the partners to reflect, in the upcoming week, on ways they fail to value their partner and ways that they devalue their partner. Close the session.

Second Session: History

Goals and Focus

This session is likely to be one of the longer of the sessions. It may take up to two hours. The personal history of each individual (including his or her spiritual history) is taken, followed by a relationship history. After histories are taken, God is called on to intervene to change the partners' memories or past hurtfulness.

Suggested Activities

Give a rationale for history-taking. Suggest that patterns of hurt established in families of origin are often repeated in later relationships. Ask each partner to describe his or her upbringing, especially ways that parents treated each other as marital partners. Those memories often form two types of ideals for present marriages—ideals of how marriages should and shouldn't be.

Explore each partner's family of origin. The pastor also inquires about ways their parents treated each person when he or she was a child. Parental hurtfulness, intentional or unintentional, often forms the template that shapes current emotional response.

Throughout the summary of each partner's family-of-origin history, direct attention to the ways that valuing was or was not shown by parents toward each partner. Perhaps each partner responded to parents by devaluing also. The pastor attempts to establish that many of the ways partners behave toward each other result from the ways that their parents often behaved toward them.

Ask about previous dating partners. The history-taking is expanded to include previous important dating relationships. Often hurts within previous relationships have made a big impact on the person. Determine patterns of valuing and devaluing in those relationships.

Trace the history of the present marriage from the time the partners met to the present. The history-taking continues with the formation of the current marriage. The dating history and the engagement are discussed. The early years of the marriage are also described. The pastor seeks opportunities to call a pattern of behavior to the partners' attention. When things were working well between the partners, they conveyed to each other that they were valuable and valued people. As the marriage relationship began to experience strain, devaluing thoughts and behaviors intruded into the relationship—until the present, in which the spouses may feel little valuing toward each other. Even if some feeling of value remains, the behaviors that each complain about are usually ones that make the other person feel devalued. Devaluing might include such things as neglect, violence, sexual abuse, alcohol, incest, put-downs, negatively labeling children, playing favorites, demonstrating that the child was not important through being unavailable, yelling, bossing, and bullying.

Promote a healing of memories. Generally, discovering the sins of the past and their continuing presence in the present is not enough. The pastor should strive for a healing of memories. Some people might respond well to visualization methods, though this must be tailored to specific client needs.

The ideal end-point of this session is to get the person to forgive the parents for the hurts of the past and to renounce the continued practice of childhood-based devaluing in the present marriage. The healing of memories can have a spiritual reality. Jesus is not bound by time and can literally go back into the past and affect the past as easily as he can affect the present or future.

Assign activities between sessions. Assign couples to read portions from *Value Your Mate* that apply to their marriage.

Important Points

It is easy to become lost in the details of people's past lives and forget the main focus of counseling, which is to identify the historical roots of current ways that failure to love shows up in the marriage. Constant attention to failures to value or to devaluing will help counselees become more capable of modifying those patterns in future interviews.

Third Session: Problem Areas in Current Marriage

Goals and Focus

By the third session, you should know which area—closeness, communication, conflict resolution, cognition, or commitment—is the major area on which intervention should concentrate. In Strategic Pastoral Marital Counseling, there is probably only enough time to deal with one main area.

Discuss problems in that area and relate them to failure to value the spouse and exercise faith working through love. Because the third session is problem-focused, it is helpful for both you and the counselees to understand that in the fourth session, the focus will be on what can be done to improve the area and to increase faith working through love in a practical way.

Suggested Activities

Blessing and cursing in marriage. Explain that marriage is built on the idea of blessing, not cursing the spouse. Blessing is building the partner up, valuing him or her. Cursing is devaluing the partner. Cursing applies the golden-plated rule: "hurt unto others as they have hurt unto you." Cursing leads to mountains of depression, bitterness, hurt, anger, and retaliation that can only be cast into the sea by faith. Faith involves seeing what *can be* as well as what *is* in the marriage. Whereas the cycle of cursing (devaluing, hurting, anger, and retaliation) drives us into the pit, the cycle of blessing (confession, repentance, and forgiveness) lifts us into the lofty heavens. Blessing breaks the cycle of cursing.

Solicit intent to bless rather than curse. After you share this concept with the individual or couple, secure the commitment to find ways to build up and value the partner rather than to curse the partner. Spouses are joint heirs of the grace of Christ, and therefore should treat each other like royalty.

Discuss the crucial area. The couple is asked to consider the area of their marriage that appears to be the most crucial. They examine that area with a special eye toward how they devalue, or curse, the spouse in their actions in that area. This may be a discouraging session because it focuses on finding negative behaviors. The emphasis must clearly be on having each partner identify what he or she does that is not helpful, rather than on identifying what he or she perceives the partner to do.

Reestablish hope. At the end of the session, help meet the couple's needs for hope in their darkness. This is a special time of providing support and hope as the couple experiences a dark moment. It is your character that can empower each person to support the other in his or her need. Further, your supportiveness is an example of Christ working through you in meeting the couple's needs.

Assign activities between sessions. Assign couples to read portions from *Value Your Mate* that apply to their marriage. Keeping partners engaged with counseling throughout the week is the key to improving the marriage.

Important Points

As with all of counseling, there is a balance between a focus on problems and a focus on solutions. Maintaining a hopeful attitude in the couple despite the focus on problems is your challenge in this session. You should contribute to the counselees' understanding of the core vision of marriage and promote a more spiritually mature way of looking at and dealing with the area.

Fourth Session: Changing Problem Areas

Goals and Focus

In this session, discuss the same major problem area that was explored in the previous session, but focus more on solutions to the problems that were uncovered in the previous session. The problem of failure to love—devaluing and failing to value—is reiterated, and the couple learns how they can show love daily.

Suggested Activities

Discuss God's plan for marriage. Ephesians 5 is discussed as the model for mutual self-sacrifice regardless of the role one is in— as husband or wife, parent or child, master or slave. People are admonished to outdo one another in showing love. Headship is described as headship in initiative at showing love and leadership at self-sacrificially blessing the spouse.

Look back at the good times. Couples are encouraged to reflect on times when they have been satisfied with their marriage. They identify ways they communicated to the partner that the partner was needed and valued. Couples are encouraged to do more of what previously worked.

Use the session for active involvement. Rather than using the session for talk, involve the couple in active learning (see Chapter 7 for descriptions of interventions). If intimacy is the major problem, have partners treat the distance across your office as representative of their feelings of closeness. Have them discuss fond memories and measure how their feelings of closeness change. If communication is the major problem, have the partners communicate. If they use poor communication, point it out and (importantly) have them correct it. If conflict resolution is the main problem, have partners tackle a disagreement. Audiotape their discussion (with their permission, of course) and use the tape recording to show them how their problem-solving gets off-track. Help them try to solve the problem using more effective problem-solving strategies. If blaming, pessimistic expectations, negative assumptions, or negative self-talk are problems, show people how to change those cognitions. If commitment is the major problem in the marriage, there are usually other problems, affecting marital satisfaction that are integrally involved—failures in intimacy, poor communication, unresolved conflict, or negative cognition. Commitment can be dealt with directly by decreasing alternatives to the marriage or by increasing investments in the marriage; or it may be dealt with indirectly through increasing marital satisfaction. Further, covenantal versus contractual views of commitment may be discussed in the session to help revise the counselees' view of marriage.

Assign activities to perform between sessions. Assign portions of *Value Your Mate* to be read and discussed prior to the final session. Whereas previous assignments from this book have been *reading* assignments, the present assignment should focus on active involvement in the area of concentration. Lasting change depends on the partners trying to change between sessions.

Besides reading and engaging in exercises, couples should reflect on aspects of their behavior that they want to confess to their partners in the final counseling session. When confession and forgiveness are discussed, partners should be prepared through prayerful self-examination.

Important Points

This session builds on the previous ones in changing patterns of devaluing to patterns of valuing and prompting the couple to exercise faith working through love. By the fourth session, the couple should already be trying to change their marriage in their time together at home. The fourth session is a chance to engage the couple in trying to make changes and to give them feedback on their efforts.

Keep a limited focus throughout the session. It is tempting to try to solve several problems during the session—especially if the couple presents many obvious problems. Resist the urge to spread yourself too thin. More will be accomplished by thoroughly addressing one or two related problems than by superficially addressing several problems.

Fifth Session: Disengagement

In the fifth session, there are a number of objectives. Develop assignments that help people retrain themselves in valuing the other person and in acting in faith working through love. Solidify attitudes of confession and forgiveness by conducting a forgiveness session. Try to get the couple involved in other church activities, which might involve working with lay couples who will continue an informal counseling relationship. Encourage the couple to participate in discipleship, support, or Bible study groups.

Suggested Activities

Have people confess their part in marital troubles to their partner. Begin the session with a question about whether the partners carried out their assignments during the week since the last meeting. Specifically, did they reflect on confessions to their spouse about their part in the marital tensions? Have partners proceed through the confession and forgiveness intervention.

Have people plan what they are going to do now. This may include discussing ways they want to continue to work on their marriage. It is usually advisable to help couples be as specific as possible about future plans. Vague plans such as "keep working on our marriage" won't usually be carried out. Have partners agree on one area to change and stick with it for several weeks, reading relevant portions of *Value Your Mate* as needed.

Planning specific actions might include referral for additional counseling. Even if counseling has been helpful, additional counseling might be necessary. Don't feel threatened if five sessions of counseling were not enough to revolutionize the marriage. Generally, problems build up over many years and will take a long time to be completely solved. You may feel pressured to move into long-term marriage counseling, but resist the urge. Be realistic about your time commitments and your full range of pastoral duties. Remind the couple of the agreement with which you began the five-session format.

Have people summarize what they have learned. Ask the couple to reflect on what they have learned. Stress the main points:

- God is the healer and sustainer of marriages.
- God's plan for marriage is faith working through love, which means actively valuing and avoiding devaluing the partner.
- "Tri*UMPH*ant marriage" requires the "UMPH" of extra effort on their part as well as reliance on God.

The Joshua intervention. People create a memorial to the Lord to commemorate his work in their marriage.

Important Points

Don't expect astounding progress in five sessions. The canoe of the marriage has been floating downstream toward the rocks and waterfall for a considerable time prior to counseling. In only five sessions, feel happy if you merely turn the canoe around. Many paddle strokes will be required to move the canoe upstream.

With only five counseling sessions, spiritual concerns will not be adequately dealt with either. Counseling provides a way of applying spiritual principles of faith working through love in a practical laboratory. Reinforce the lessons that the individuals have learned throughout counseling—that Christianity is faith working through love. Further, marriage, like Christianity, is about valuing others, caring enough to place others' needs above one's own.

The parishioner learns additional lessons through the ministry of the local church. True discipleship takes place as the local church nurtures the pattern of faith working through love in its preaching, fellowship, small groups, and Christian education. The ministry of the church is to produce mature Christian disciples. Marital counseling is only one small piece of the entire pattern.

11

Case Examples

It is tempting to think that effective Strategic Pastoral Marital Counseling can occur if you're simply well prepared.

It's not that simple.

Even if you have sufficient knowledge about theology and marriage, rich experience in counseling, a good strategy (such as promoting faith working through love), a five-session plan, and excellent ideas about interventions, you need more. The best counselors have a gentleness that communicates love and firmness, and the best Christian counselors combine that with openness to the leading of the Holy Spirit.

Unfortunately, these personal qualities cannot be conveyed through a book. We can talk *about* them, but unless the pastor stands humble and broken before the Lord, counseling may be mechanical and ineffective.

In a sense, this book—like all books—can address only the mechanics of counseling. The heart of counseling is within, as the working of the Holy Spirit flows from the pastor like a river of living water. Effective counseling is truly dealing with a person or a couple in love and truth, from the heart.

162

Application

Yet it is our responsibility, as ministers of Jesus Christ's gospel, that we prepare—through reading, studying, and training—to counsel, to the best of our God-given ability, those whom God leads to us.

To complete the preparation that we can offer through this book, we describe three partial cases that illustrate difficulties that are encountered in Strategic Pastoral Marital Counseling. The first case describes counseling a woman whose husband is uninterested in attending counseling. The second case involves a couple, with both partners Christian, who attend counseling together. The third case involves a couple who attend counseling together but only one partner is a Christian.

An Individual: Virginia

Background

Virginia and Paul had been married three years. Both were devoted Christians who had attended the same church for five years. They met in the adult Sunday school class, attended premarital counseling with the pastor, and married after dating for eighteen months.

Virginia had come to the church in the midst of depression. By the time she met Paul, Virginia—aged 25—had been in conflict with her father and mother for seven years. She became depressed when her father died suddenly.

Paul had grown up in Richmond. At 38 years old, when he met Virginia, he had never been married; nor had he ever dated anyone for an extended period.

Virginia was immediately attracted to Paul's maturity and experience as a Christian. Depressed, she fell hard for "an older man," as she jokingly referred to him, who cared for her and helped her through her emotional nadir. Paul responded to Virginia's neediness, attention, and youthfulness. He felt "wise," "useful," and "important" in her presence. They married after Virginia broke out of the depression.

After three years of marriage, though, they began to argue—at first about different bed times, then about sex. Within a few months, they argued about almost any topic that they discussed. Virginia moved into the guest room and slept on the sofa sleeper. She continued to attend church regularly; Paul attended only sporadically. Six months later, Virginia sought counseling from her pastor.

Counseling

Virginia explained the problem and her pastor listened carefully. He quickly assessed the main problems to be centered around conflict and intimacy. Additionally, much of the problem seemed to be Paul's questioning of his faith, which had led him to change his lifestyle and question other fundamental values.

After the first session with Virginia alone, their pastor called Paul and asked if he would attend counseling with Virginia. He said that he didn't think the problems were that serious. After an extended phone conversation with the pastor, Paul still refused to attend. He became angry when the pastor suggested that Paul's faith might need attention.

During the second session, Virginia described her past conflicts with her father and her inability to reconcile with her father due to his untimely death. The pastor prayed with her for a healing of memories, and Virginia wept long, wracking sobs as she confessed her hurtfulness of her parents. She resolved to reestablish a relationship with her still-estranged mother. During the marital history, the pastor came to understand Virginia as a needy woman, driven by guilt to marry a substitute for her father, who did not live up to what she had anticipated prior to marriage. Paul was not the caring, warm father she had thought him to be when they dated. In fact, she said, "He frequently becomes angry over nothing, lashing out with the most hateful, bitter things. I've learned to fight back, not like the first year of our marriage, when I was still depressed and he could push me around and intimidate me. He hasn't liked it very much since I began to stand up for myself."

The pastor helped Virginia see that Paul and she had been attracted to each other for many reasons, and for a while, those reasons kept them happy. She said she wanted to recapture those times and pledged her willingness to work hard to bring the marriage back together.

That Sunday, their pastor and his wife were at a local restaurant, when strains of a heated conversation floated across the dining area. Paul and Virginia were seated two tables away, engrossed in a dispute, unaware of the pastor's presence.

Virginia said, " . . . can't trust you to do anything right. I gave you the tickets, and I thought that I could trust you to keep up with them until Sunday night. But no. It's like giving something to an irresponsible kid."

"I'm sorry. I thought I put them with my coat."

"Yeah, you're sorry, but now we have to drive all the way home and search for the things. We're going to be late, and you know it always embarrasses me to walk into something like this late. If I didn't know better, I'd say you were trying to do this on purpose."

"I said I'm sorry. I didn't do it on purpose."

"Well, it's either that or you're incompetent. It is a royal pain being married to you. You're just a boy in a man's body, and sometimes I wonder whether it's even a functioning man's body."

Paul wiped his hand over his eyes, and pinched the bridge of his nose. He sighed. "Honey, you know I'd make love any time you want. You just . . . "

"I don't want to. I couldn't stand to be touched by you." Virginia jerked the napkin from her lap, stood and stalked out. Paul fished in his back pocket for his billfold, dropped a few dollars on the table, and carried the check to the cash register.

The pastor turned back to his wife as Paul and Virginia exited. "Wow," said the pastor's wife. "That is one venomous woman."

"I think I've made a few errors," said the pastor, "but at least I have some time to repair them."

Lessons for Pastoral Counseling

Indeed, the pastor had made several errors that occur sometimes when only one partner is counseled.

- The pastor had relied on only one source of information.
- Without knowing it, he formed an alliance with Virginia because he saw only her story.

- He empowered her and might have even impelled her toward divorce by his hearing only her story.
- He could not affect Paul's behavior directly because Paul was not in counseling. He could only affect Virginia's behavior and thereby hope to influence the marriage indirectly.
- He did not know how Virginia's behavior was being perceived by Paul.

In the subsequent sessions, the pastor confronted Virginia about her style of conflict and her anger. Further, he called Paul again and asked whether he was willing to attend counseling. The pastor's manner apparently helped convince Paul that it would be useful for the partners to attend counseling together. The couple were seen for five sessions together, then referred to a local Christian marriage counselor for additional marriage counseling.

In the event of counseling only one marriage partner, you must vigilantly avoid being drawn into an unwitting coalition with the person who is being counseled. It is easy to empathize with the person who presents his or her painful story. But there are two sides to every story, so remain on guard against casting the absent spouse as the villain.

A Christian Couple: Julie and Lawrence

A Counselor's Nightmare

In the fourth session of marital counseling with Julie and Lawrence, their pastor faced one of the moments that nightmares are made of. He had just worked for an hour with Lawrence and Julie concerning their intimacy. Lawrence was a rational, reasonable, nonemotional man. Julie was emotional and volatile. They were engaged in a classic distancer-pursuer pattern, with Julie demanding more intimacy and Lawrence trying to avoid her emotional demands. The pastor had worked for two weeks on their intimacy. Then Julie dropped the first bombshell.

"It was tough being in the room with two super-rational males," she said. "I felt like everything had to be so, so, well, so rational. I felt stifled."

"That's the way she usually is," said Lawrence while the pastor was still reeling from Julie's criticism. "She's not very submissive. Whenever she has to be submissive, it galls her, and she whines about it. Pastor, you need to straighten her out about her role as a submissive wife." Lawrence had dropped the second bombshell.

Julie quickly said, "I've done a lot of reading about submission. I think Lawrence misinterprets the sense of the whole Scripture in focusing on the passage in Ephesians as establishing a hierarchy within the home. Don't you agree, Pastor?"

The pastor was stunned. Over the years, he had found counseling Christian couples to be advantageous in many ways:

- Partners share important values and beliefs.
- Both perspectives are available.
- Communication can be seen, not just talked about.
- The tendency to form alliances is diminished.

Yet in the current case, he faced two of the greatest dilemmas of counseling Christians, simultaneously.

The Dilemmas

One is the theological tug-of-war. The pastor can get caught in the middle on theological issues and be thrust into the role of referee who decides which of the partners is theologically correct. The pastor is seen as usually more expert theologically than the typical layperson. If the pastor takes sides—especially if the issue has been a longstanding one—then the counseling relationship can be compromised.

The second is the gender tug-of-war. The pastor, male or female, obviously is of one gender, and tension can be created in both partners. The person of same sex as the pastor may feel that the pastor will understand him or her better and may assume a coalition that may not, in fact, exist. This can lead to disappointment and unfulfilled expectations. On the other hand, the person of different gender than the pastor may feel ganged up on, which can also harm the counseling relationship.

Toward Solutions

Solving the theological tug-of-war can present difficult questions for the pastor. In general, avoid thinking of theological disputes as *merely* questions about theology. Although they are about theology, they have a function in the relationship between spouses and can affect the partners' relationship with the pastor. When asked to decide a disputed point of theology between partners, think first of keeping the books balanced. If you decide to favor one person's position over the other's, ask yourself about what issue you intend to support the other person on.

People often believe that counselors are supposed to remain neutral and not offer an opinion on a dispute. Yet counselor neutrality is a misunderstanding of counseling. All counselors at times support the position of one spouse over that of the other spouse *if* one position is clearly better than the other. However, counselors also must balance their influence to prevent one spouse from feeling unsupported and judged.

Often the easiest way out of the dilemma is to present an interpretation of the disputed scriptural passage that is different from that of either partner. That allows the pastor to remain true to his or her own interpretation of Scripture while not disrupting the balance of power within the marriage.

At other times, when the theological dispute is clearly a bid to co-opt the pastor into a power coalition, it is best to avoid answering the question. You might say, "I think that is an important issue, but I'd rather not deal with that at the present time. It might just make things worse. Before we end counseling, I'll give you my interpretation but for now let's tackle a different issue."

The gender tug-of-war is becoming increasingly prevalent as the women's movement has gained prominence. People are sensitized to gender differences, and they often see gender prejudice where there is none. On the other hand, people often are unaware of their own prejudices, so it pays to remain open to avoiding unintentional biases. If you are challenged on a prejudice, examine your behavior nondefensively and be willing to admit mistakes.

Today, in a climate of heightened awareness of gender issues, the best way to handle gender differences is usually to address them openly at the earliest part of counseling. Admit that you are a male or female and acknowledge that you intend to work hard to make sure that doesn't affect counseling. By acknowledging your gender explicitly, you prevent each person from entertaining fantasies about establishing a coalition for or against him or her.

A Couple with One Christian Partner: Roberta and Ronnie

Background

Ronnie and Roberta had been married for 15 years. Both Ronnie and Roberta had lived without reference to religion for all 15 years of marriage. Neither had gone to church since adolescence. Ronnie was reared as a member of the Disciples of Christ. Roberta had grown up in a family that occasionally went to synagogue but were essentially uninvolved with their Jewish faith.

Then Ronnie was converted to Christianity.

Conflict over religion became daily fare. Ronnie became involved in a local Methodist church, and Roberta complained bitterly that he had abandoned her and their three middle and high school children. As conflict increased, both partners became increasingly distressed. Ronnie asked Roberta to attend marital counseling with the pastor of his church. At first, she counter-proposed that they attend counseling with a secular counselor, but after investigating the cost of counseling and examining their checkbook balance, she decided to attend counseling at the Methodist church.

Counseling

The pastor, herself a product of a mixed marriage between a theologically liberal Roman Catholic and a fundamentalist Baptist, was sympathetic to Roberta's discomfort. At the beginning of counseling, Pastor Sontag related her own background and talked of the struggles she had seen in her own family of origin. She invited Roberta to share her worries. Roberta disclosed her fears about being ganged up on, and Pastor Sontag assured Roberta that she would make a special effort not to impose her values on Roberta.

On the other hand, Pastor Sontag clearly stated that her view of marriage was one that was informed by Scripture and that she held a high view of marriage and a belief that marriage was meant to be a commitment for life.

Roberta agreed with Pastor Sontag's understanding of marriage as a permanent commitment, and agreed to counseling. She stipulated, though, that no attempt be made to convert her to Christianity.

Pastor Sontag said, "Roberta, I cannot promise that I won't want you to meet Jesus. I believe that he is the way to true happiness. But I believe everyone has the right and responsibility to choose that for herself, and I can assure you that if you don't ask me to tell you more about Jesus, I won't impose on you. How does that sound?"

Roberta said, "That sounds like the best thing I've heard since Ronnie became a Christian—a promise that I won't be told 15 times a day that I need to accept Jesus as my personal Savior. If I want to know more, I'll ask you—or Ronnie."

After church the following Sunday, Ronnie accosted Pastor Sontag after others had gone. "Pastor Sontag, I heard what you said to Roberta in counseling, and I didn't mention anything at the time, but I wanted to ask what you thought. Do you think I'm pushing too hard about Roberta's need for Christ?"

Pastor Sontag said, "What has her reaction been?"

"She doesn't listen to anything I say. She turns me off."

"Then, are you being an effective witness by continuing to bring up something she has asked you not to talk about?"

"No, but I love her and want her to be saved."

"Have you told her of that concern?"

"Yeah, lots."

"Then, if you think she has heard you—which I think she has—you might give her some room. Peter gives advice to women in 1 Peter 3, saying that they should win their husbands to Jesus 'without a word' with their reverent and chaste behavior. I think the same principle applies here. You need to show her the love of Jesus rather than preach to her. You've already preached to her. If she sees a love in you that she wants, she'll ask."

"How about the conflict we seem to have again and again over whether I spend too much time around church? What do you think?"

"How you use your time is something the two of you will work out as we go through counseling. Let me say, though, what I'm sure is obvious to you. Being around church is not the same thing as serving the Lord. I think that you and Roberta need to work out a balance in that area."

Important Considerations

Counseling the mixed religious couple involves several considerations.

- Special care is needed not to collude with the Christian spouse, while you remain true to your Christian values.
- The pastor needs to be clear on how and when witnessing to the non-Christian is appropriate. Guidelines will likely differ for different couples. One rule of thumb, though, is that the couple rarely comes to counseling to be witnessed to. Witnesses are *summoned* to testify. If the non-Christian wants to hear the witness, he or she will usually make it clear that the witness is being summoned. Like Pastor Sontag, the pastor should clearly be identified as a Christian who is guided by Christian faith and love, and the invitation to share the testimony should be available if requested.
- The pastor must have guidance on how to deal with a spouse who thinks his or her partner is devoting too much time and energy to religious activities.

One final issue is important. The pastor must decide how to conceptualize the marital problem in a way that doesn't turn the non-Christian off. Conceiving of the problem as deficiencies in love—too little valuing or too much active devaluing of the partner—is a way to guide the couple using Christian principles without using too much Christian vocabulary.

With the mixed religious marriage, as with all marriages, God is working. The pastor is an agent to promote love and discipleship and can be used by God to the extent that he or she approaches the partners with love and responsible preparation.

Self-Righteousness in the Unequally Yoked Couple

The principle of faith working through love applies to the unequally yoked couple and to marriages in which only one partner is active in church. Christians who talk their faith without living out the pattern of the Scriptures can push their partners farther from Christ. Spiritual pride, false assumptions about a partner's sin in comparison to one's own holiness, nagging in the name of Jesus, and ignoring the spouse by overinvolvement in church activities— all can build up resentment in the spouse. These are the opposite of faith working through love. They are ways that Christian people devalue non-Christian people.

Try to spot such unloving patterns and gently challenge the Christian partner to practice Christian love toward his or her spouse. When the non-Christian sees a genuine pattern of maturity and love growing up in the Christian, he or she is most likely to have a change of heart toward God. It is the pattern itself that bears witness to the non-Christian spouse. Discipleship creates more disciples, because the pattern of faith working through love brings integrity to the name of Christ.

A Sincere Christian in an Unequally Yoked Marriage

When the Christian spouse is genuinely living out the pattern of Christian maturity by truly loving the partner into the kingdom, then the question often becomes, how can the Christian keep on loving the partner despite a lack of response? How can a Christian practice love in the midst of hostility, rebellion, unresponsiveness, and testing? This situation seems hard beyond measure. Yet this is precisely the challenge that Jesus sometimes gives to the Christian spouse.

In these situations, the pastor can pray with the Christian partner for the power of God's love to meet every need. "Love your enemy" and "Return good for evil" are perhaps the hardest words in the Bible, and are supremely tested in the marital arena—especially in the unequally yoked couple.

Most of the time, the pastor avoids taking sides on marital problems because those problems often come from people's carnal nature, and we must avoid allying ourselves with anyone's carnal nature. But where a parishioner sincerely desires to crucify the carnal nature, to die to self, and to love the partner into the kingdom, the pastor *must* align himself or herself with the mature Christian spirit within that person.

A decision to love a non-Christian person is an extraordinary work of the Holy Spirit, a genuine product of divine inspiration. We must remember then that faith working through love is a different pattern than simply "love each other." It calls Christians to depend on Jesus for our self-esteem, so that we can overlook marital hurts that bring anger, defensiveness, and blame. Faith working through love implies that it is possible to love people because of God's love for us—which we receive by faith. This type of love can grow even when it is not reciprocated.

Nevertheless, a person who has committed himself or herself to this kind of love needs all the support possible. Once a pastor has determined that his or her parishioner is moving beyond self-righteousness, the pastor can support the parishioner by faithful prayer, encouragement, and caring love—without taking sides against the non-Christian partner. While forming a supportive alliance, he or she can love both partners equally—recognizing that Jesus died for both and that God loves both.

The Reward of Christ's Love

This is not to say, either, that the non-Christian spouse will finally come to the Lord. Paul's words in 1 Corinthians 7:16 cannot be easily swept away: "How do you know, wife, whether you will save your husband? Or, how do you know, husband, whether you will save your wife?" Regardless of the outcome, God is pleased by faithfulness and love, and mature Christianity is its own reward. God is not limited in the ways of rewarding faithfulness. He can find other ways of rewarding faithfulness besides converting spouses—and conversion must be left to God's hands.

Our job is not to convert people, but to disciple them, teaching them to observe what Jesus commanded. We leave conversion to God and pay attention to our God-given work. If we have helped strengthen a parishioner to accomplish the heroism of true love, we have accomplished something really great, something eternal, something pleasing and heroic in God's eyes.

Conclusion

We began the book with Pastor Dennis, who felt inadequate in counseling Marla and Les. We end having come full circle. The pastor who is a successful counselor knows that he or she *is* inadequate to affect permanent change in marriage or in people's spiritual lives. Yet we know that Jesus Christ is not inadequate, and he has provided us with the awesome responsibility of being his body and, when he calls us, of working through us.

References

Arnold, J. D., and C. Schick. 1979. Counseling by clergy: A review of empirical research. *Journal of Pastoral Counseling* 14(2): 76–101.

Baucom, D. H., and N. Epstein. 1990. *Cognitive-behavioral marital therapy*. New York: Brunner/Mazel.

Benner, David G. 1992. *Strategic pastoral counseling: A short-term structured model*. Grand Rapids: Baker.

Berry, J. T. 1991. Coping with sexual attraction at work: A study of psychotherapists, ministers, and personnel managers. Unpublished diss., Virginia Commonwealth University, Richmond.

Beutler, L. E., M. Crago, and T. G. Arizmendi. 1986. Research on therapist variables in psychotherapy. In *Handbook of psychotherapy and behavior change*, ed. S. L. Garfield and A. E. Bergin, 3d ed. 257–310. New York: Wiley.

Bordin, E. S. 1979. The generalizability of the psychoanalytic concept of the working alliance. *Psychotherapy: Theory, Research and Practice* 16: 252–60.

Bromley, D. G., and B. C. Busching. 1988. Understanding the structure of contractual and covenantal social relations: Implications for the sociology of religion. *Sociological Analysis* 49: 15–32.

Bumpass, L. L., J. A. Sweet, and A. J. Cherlin. 1991. The role of cohabitation in declining rates of marriage. *Journal of Marriage and the Family* 53: 913–27.

175

Cherlin, A. J. 1981. *Marriage, divorce, remarriage*. Cambridge, Mass.: Harvard University Press.

DeMaris, A., and V. Rao. 1992. Premarital cohabitation and subsequent marital stability in the United States: A reassessment. *Journal of Marriage and the Family* 54: 178–90.

deShazer, S. 1988. *Clues: Investigating solutions in brief therapy*. New York: W. W. Norton.

Fisher, R., and W. Ury. 1981. *Getting to yes: Negotiating agreement without giving in*. New York: Penguin.

Goldsmith, W. M., and B. K. Hansen. 1991. Boundary areas of religious clients' values: Target for therapy. *Journal of Psychology and Christianity* 10: 224–36.

Gottman, J. 1979. *Empirical investigations of marriage*. New York: Academic Press.

Gurin, G., J. Veroff, and S. Feld. 1960. *Americans view their mental health*. New York: Basic Books.

Lasswell, M., and T. Lasswell. 1991. *Marriage and the family*. 3d ed. Belmont, Calif.: Wadsworth.

Malony, H. N. 1988. The clinical assessment of optimal religious functioning. *Review of Religious Research* 30(1): 2–17.

Marsden, G. M. 1990. *Religion and American culture*. San Diego: Harcourt Brace Jovanovich.

Mayton, K. I. 1989. The stress-buffering role of spiritual support: Cross-sectional and prospective investigations. *Journal for the Scientific Study of Religion* 28: 310–23.

McMurry, Douglas. 1983. *Bread! An invitation to the Christian Life*. Hillsboro, Oreg.: Bethlehem Books.

———. 1985. *Food groups: A Balanced diet for Christian growth*. Richmond Va.: Bethlehem Books.

Minuchin, S., and H. C. Fishman. 1981. *Family therapy techniques*. Cambridge, Mass.: Harvard University Press.

Orlinsky, D. E., and K. I. Howard. 1986. Process and outcome in psychotherapy. In *Handbook of psychotherapy and behavior change*, ed. S. L. Garfield and A. E. Bergin, 3d ed., 311–81. New York: Wiley.

Penner, J. I., and C. L. Penner. 1990. *Counseling for sexual disorders*. Dallas: Word.

Pittman, F. 1989. *Private lies: Infidelity and the betrayal of intimacy.* New York: W. W. Norton.

Rogers, C. R. 1951. *Client-centered therapy.* Boston: Houghton-Mifflin.

————. 1957. The necessary and sufficient conditions of therapeutic personality change. *Journal of Consulting Psychology* 21: 95–103.

Schaefer, M. T., and D. H. Olson. 1981. Assessing intimacy: The PAIR inventory. *Journal of Marital and Family Therapy* 7: 47–60.

Schoen, R. 1992. First unions and the stability of marriages. *Journal of Marriage and the Family* 54: 281–84.

Seamands, D. A. 1985. *Healing of memories.* Wheaton, Ill.: Victor Books.

Shackelford, J. F, ed. 1989. Sexual affairs: Special issue. *Journal of Psychology and Christianity* 8(4): 5–72.

Strupp, H. H., S. W. Hadley, and B. Gomez-Schwartz. 1977. *Psychotherapy for better or worse.* New York: Jason Aronson.

Stuart, R. B. 1980. *Helping couples change: A social learning approach to marital therapy.* New York: Guilford.

Thompson, E., and U. Colella. 1992. Cohabitation and marital stability: Quality or commitment? *Journal of Marriage and the Family* 54: 259–67.

U.S. Bureau of the Census. 1984. *Census of population: General social and economic characteristics.* Washington, D.C.: U.S. Government Printing Office.

Veroff, J., R. A. Kulka, and E. Douvan. 1981. *Mental health in America: Patterns of help-seeking from 1957 to 1976.* New York: Basic Books.

Walsh, F. 1991. Promoting healthy functioning in divorced and remarried families. In *Handbook of family therapy,* ed. A. S. Gurman and D. P. Kniskern, 525–45. New York: Brunner/Mazel.

Worthington, E. L., Jr. 1986. Religious counseling: A review of published empirical research. *Journal of Counseling and Development* 64: 421–31.

————. 1989. *Marriage counseling: A Christian approach to counseling couples.* Downers Grove, Ill.: InterVarsity.

————. 1990. *Counseling before marriage.* Dallas: Word.

————. 1991. Marriage counseling with Christian couples. In *Case studies in Christian counseling*, ed. G. R. Collins, 72–99. Dallas: Word.

Worthington, E. L., Jr., and F. A. DiBlasio. 1990. Promoting mutual forgiveness within the fractured relationship. *Psychotherapy* 27: 219–23.

Worthington, E. L., Jr., P. A. Dupont, J. T. Berry, and L. A. Duncan. 1988. Christian therapists' and clients' perceptions of religious psychotherapy in private and agency settings. *Journal of Psychology and Theology* 16: 282–93.

Wuthnow, R. 1988. *The restructuring of American religion: Society and faith since World War II*. Princeton, N.J.: Princeton University Press.